Lorallyn

I DEARLY/ APPRECIATE YOU,

Ruth

THE
TRIP TO
FREEDOM

How I walked through the door to freedom using God's
Word after forty-five years of horrific abuse

Ruth Johnson

THE TRIP TO FREEDOM
Third Edition – December 2015
Second Edition – September 2005
First Edition – January 1998

ISBN: 978-0-9661470-4-9
Copyright © 2015 Lighthouse of Hope Publications

Published by:
Lighthouse of Hope Publications
914 164th Street S.E. #B-12 PMB #365
Mill Creek, Washington, U.S.A. 98012-6339

WHO THIS BOOK WILL HELP

A note from the Author

For all those who long to stop the hurts from your painful past, but you have not found answers that help you in a lasting way, I assure you that in this book you will find Word-based truths and they **do** work. They **can** set you free.

The many practical insights also can protect any single, including the younger generation who are at the beginning of their journey of discovering who they want to date, from the suffering I experienced in destructive relationships. This is how a young person felt about reading this book:

"I think "The Trip to Freedom" will definitely help people, including the youth, to understand what to look for in someone when they are dating so that they don't have to learn the hard way, after they've already damaged their life." Koenn Becker

Finally, this book was written to help young people who are struggling and you don't understand how to overcome what is troubling you. I want you to know that it means everything to me to be able to help you while you are still young so that you don't lose the years I lost trying to find my way to all this radically life-changing understanding. Many of you are part of a fatherless generation and in "The Trip to Freedom" you will personally encounter God as a very real Father and the caring Dad you missed out on. You will also find blunt honesty about my own struggles and this will help you to find comfort, reassurance and peace.

THE SCRIPTURES IN

"THE TRIP TO FREEDOM"

The verses in this book are the same ones I personalized when I was on my journey of getting set free.

Looking at them in such a life-changing way is actually what helped me the most to see God for the first time as an incredibly loving Father.

ACKNOWLEDGMENTS

My husband, Barry

Barry encouraged me every step of the way in this rewrite of the original 1998 "Trip to Freedom." Often it was his kind, encouraging support that spurred me on in this major undertaking. I'm deeply grateful for him believing so strongly in the importance of this book being significantly updated so that it now could be far more effective in helping singles of all ages.

Koenn Becker

Koenn has an amazing gift in Graphic Arts. He actually designed the amazing book cover as a freshman in high school. I'm so thankful for the help of this special young man so that the message of hope in "The Trip to Freedom" could be so powerfully captured on the cover.

THE CHAPTERS

Chapter One

THERE IS HOPE

Everyone needs to be genuinely loved. It is the deepest longing of the human soul. Yet some people choose relationships in which this love is not possible.

They might even tell themselves, and really mean it:

> "Never again will I get involved with someone who is not capable of loving me.
>
> Never again am I going to let anyone abuse me."

Then they do exactly what they promised themselves they would never do and end up in another destructive relationship.

For most people who struggle with being drawn to those who are a mistake to be friends with or date, this issue usually started when they were a child. If we didn't have a dad or mom who loved us when we were very young, we have a painful hole in our heart. We will never be completely free of the damage from that loss until our need for the love of a father or mother is met.

Yet as adults, we can't look to our earthly parents to provide this love because they may never be able to have a healthy, supportive relationship with us.

Therefore if we base our getting set free on that change taking place, we will remain stuck in our pain. We will also continue to be attracted to those who will mistreat us, all in a futile effort to fill the emptiness in our heart.

In my own search for freedom, my breakthrough began when I started to realize that only a personal encounter with God's Word and growing in understanding His kind Father's love could set me free from the torment of my pain.

What's absolutely remarkable is that the more I was changed by this new way of thinking, the more that unhealthy people no longer even liked me because I had stopped allowing others to mistreat me in any personal relationship.

These were amazing changes that were overwhelmingly worth *whatever* really hard choices I had to make so that they could become possible.

My hope and prayer is that what you are about to read can truly help you find your own path to freedom.

Chapter Two

I NEEDED JESUS

The catalyst for every breakthrough I was ever able to experience came from what I found in God's Word, just He reassures us in these encouraging words:

"I sent My Word into your life to heal you and deliver you from your destruction."
Psalm 107:20 NASB, Psalm 119:32 NIV

However, before any scripture could help me, I had to find Jesus. This is how that happened.

I was the third of five children in an Irish Catholic family. My family lived in the poorest section of South Boston across from a soot-blackened factory and an abandoned, rat infested bus barn. Our home was in a cramped tenement with only cold water and no heat. Each day I lived in dread of the frequent encounters with rats and swarming cockroaches that were everywhere.

We never did things together. Although we were all hurting, we didn't talk about our feelings. Even during the hard times, we remained distant and didn't help each other. I longed for us to be close. But I always felt alone.

My first troubling memory occurred the day I began kindergarten.

I was excited about starting school. Yet I was also uneasy. St. Bridgett's was a long way from home and I had never been that far by myself. "Mama will go with me," I comforted myself as I watched my older brother and sister leave without me. I gulped down breakfast and quickly put on my uniform. Dressed and eager to go, I sat on the edge of a frayed brown couch and anxiously waited for my mother to appear.

"I'm not going with you," she yelled from her bedroom. I panicked.

"But Mom," I pleaded with her, as I walked frantically toward her room. "I don't know my way. Please come with me. I'm too scared to go by myself."

"I don't feel good," she responded coldly as she slammed the door. "You'll have to go alone."

None of my desperate pleas convinced her to change her mind. Stiffening with fear, I stood nervously outside her closed door and shuddered at the thought of finding my way to school on my own.

I didn't want to miss out on my first day of kindergarten. So after a long, distressing silence, I forced myself to leave and walked briskly down the street. When I could no longer see our house, I ran as fast as I could until it hurt too much to breathe.

"I hope I don't get lost," I kept telling myself. Finally I turned a corner and sighed with relief. St. Bridgett's was up ahead. I slowed my pace and tried my very best to calm down. Yet the closer I walked toward the front entrance, the more anxious I became. I hoped to catch a glimpse of my older brother and sister. That would have been so reassuring. But I couldn't see them anywhere.

Tentatively I approached the school office and was relieved when an older nun motioned to me to follow her. Moments later she left me standing at the open door of a crowded classroom.

As I looked around at all the new faces, some of the children were crying. They clung to their mothers who held them close.

"I wish Mom were here," I said to myself as tears stung my cheeks. "I wish her arms were around me. I'd feel so much better." I stared forlornly at the others for what seemed like a very long time. Then a young nun settled us in our seats and the moms reluctantly waved goodbye.

Somehow I got through those painful hours. But the sadness I felt never left me. In many ways, being a child ended for me that day because I realized I couldn't trust anyone to help me, ever again. No matter how frightening a thought this was, I knew I had to make sure that I now took care of myself.

There was one bright spot in my childhood. When I was six years old I had an encounter with God while I was kneeling at the altar of St. Bridgett's Church. He gave me this promise: "You will do something special with your life to serve Me." I never forgot those words. No matter how much I hurt, I was strengthened by the sense of purpose and destiny they gave me. So I hid this dream in my heart and every time I thought about it, I experienced a comforting hope for a different life some day.

But despite how much this encouraged me, there were so many troubling moments in our family that troubled me and gave me a heavy heart.

One of the most difficult times was the evening meal.

We ate in tense silence. Mom sat stiffly at the end of the old wooden table and positioned her tightly clenched fists on both sides of her plate. "Shut up!" she screeched at all of us if we made the slightest noise. I winced at the sound of her shrill voice. Inevitably my stomach hurt and I could hardly wait for the meal to end so that I could escape into my room.

After dinner my mother usually stayed alone in the kitchen. I often stood at a distance and watched her lean over the sink while she buried her face in her arms and moaned. I wanted so much to put my arms around her and tell her I loved her. One night I tried.

"Mom, are you alright?" I said as I walked uncertainly into the kitchen. "Is there anything I can...?"

"Get out of here!" she screamed at me before I could even finish speaking.

"But Mom," I pleaded. "Shut up and get out of here!" she yelled as she whirled around and harshly glared at me. "Leave me alone!"

I did leave her alone. But I ached inside because I could never show her how much I cared that she was hurting so terribly.

As I grew older, Mom became increasingly more despondent. Late one afternoon I heard her loud sobs and rushed into the kitchen. She was sprawled on the floor crying hysterically.

"What's wrong?" I asked with a frightened voice. "Please tell me what's wrong!"

She just shook her head at me as if to say, "Leave me alone," and kept sobbing uncontrollably.

14

"Please talk to me," I begged her as I put my hand gently on her shoulder. But she pulled away from me and couldn't speak. I ran to a neighbor's house and banged frantically on the front door. Minutes later I heard sirens approaching and an ambulance stopped at our house. Two men ran into the kitchen, strapped my mother to a stretcher. She screamed as they took her away.

No one in our family talked about what happened to Mom that day. This silence made her leaving me all the more disturbing. I fell asleep every night wondering if she would ever come back. Eventually she did, but she was even sadder. Now she lay in her bed all day long with a cold, wet washcloth covering her eyes and insisted that we keep our house dark all the time. Every shade had to be pulled down tight to block out any glimmer of sunlight.

At times I longed for someone to hold me and hug me, but there was no affection in our family. Most nights I lay in the dark shadows of my room and cried myself to sleep. Whenever I saw other little girls having fun with their mothers, I longingly dreamed of the day when Mom and I could be like that. "Maybe today we can spend some time together," I often said to myself on the way home from school. "Maybe today she will be alright."

But she was never alright.

"Leave me alone!" she screamed at me almost every afternoon as soon as I walked into the house. "Get out of here and leave me alone!" she yelled if I ever tried to say hello to her. "And don't make any noise. I want it quiet."

I could hardly wait for the days when Mom walked to the grocery store.

The second she disappeared around the corner, I pulled up all the shades and opened the windows. Cheery sunlight flooded our home and I sang the entire time she was gone. But as soon as I heard her coming up the steps, I stopped singing, rushed to close the windows and pulled down the shades.

Life went dark again.

My father was a tall man with bright blue eyes that had a lighthearted twinkle. Yet it hurt to love Pop. I never knew when he would disappear or how long he would be away.

He also had a stormy relationship with my older sister, Margie. Although I tried harder and harder to be good in order to gain Pop's approval, she didn't care about that. So she was always getting in trouble. By the time she started high school, my parents couldn't control her.

Late one evening I heard her angry screams coming from my parents' bedroom. I ran to their room. Mom was forcing my sister to lay on the bed while Pop beat her all over her body with his thick leather belt.

"Stop! Please stop!" I begged as I stood in the doorway.

They ignored me as Pop hit my sister over and over while I watched helplessly and sobbed. A year later she was taken from our family and placed in an orphanage.

Margie never came back to live with us.

In the midst of all this unhappiness, God was my only Friend. I talked to Him about everything. He was the only One who ever helped me to feel that someone cared about me. When I sang my own songs to Him, I sensed His presence close to me.

By the time I was in eighth grade, I was painfully aware of the distance between my father and me. I wanted more than anything in the world to be close to him. But I never could bridge the dark, widening chasm between us. In an effort to get closer to him, I decided to start a new bedtime tradition. I would kiss him on the cheek and hug him every night before I went to bed. But my being affectionate with Pop was uncomfortable for him. He always flinched and pulled back from me when I tried to kiss him on the cheek. But I refused to let his revulsion deter me. Instead, I told myself:

> "Even if Pop doesn't return my affection, I will still give mine to him. Showing him I love him is better than no one in the family loving anyone at all."

It comforted me to at least give love, though I never received any. But this meant I had to teach myself not to hope for that to ever happen and that choice began a sick acceptance of one sided caring that caused abusive people to be drawn to me. I also harbored a confusing anger toward my father. Something felt very wrong, but I didn't understand what it was. Then late one evening my emotions exploded into a fit of rage.

"I hate you, Pop!" I screamed as I stood facing him in the middle of the living room. "I hate you!"

He only stared at me with silent agony in his eyes as if to say, "I deserve to be despised."

When my outburst ended, he just quietly walked away from me with his shoulders stooped over like those of a broken, defeated man. I immediately regretted hurting him. I never wanted to hate my father. I needed him.

My friendship with God continued to be the only part of my life that gave me any peace. I thought a lot about doing whatever I could because He had been so good to me. So when I was fifteen, I felt that God was asking me to dedicate my life to serving Him. As a young Catholic girl, the only possible way to do that was to become a nun.

Throughout my years in high school my thoughts and plans centered on this happening and a month after graduation the day to enter the convent arrived. Pop's health was too weak for him to make the trip with me. He stood on the same weather-beaten porch where I had spent so many hours alone as a little girl as I hugged him goodbye, without him saying a word. While the car slowly made its way down the street, tears blurred my vision as I waved at Pop through the back window as he disappeared from view.

Grief engulfed me. I never really knew my father. Now our time together as father and daughter was over. Yet I didn't want this loss to spoil my happiness about becoming a nun. So I hurriedly wiped away my tears and turned my focus to what was ahead of me.

"I have a new life to look forward to now," I confidently reminded myself. "Everything's going to be alright."

The miles raced by and I was in awe of the peaceful beauty of the grounds when we finally drove into the long, graveled driveway of the Dominican Motherhouse. The only sound I could hear was the chorus of birds in the branches of the trees overhead.

"Surely here I will be happy," I told myself as I looked around at my new home. We slowly walked up a long flight of freshly painted steps and knocked on a massive wooden door.

An older nun slowly opened it. She brusquely motioned to my family to wait for me in an austerely furnished parlor while I was taken to another room where the nuns had set out my new clothes. When I rejoined my family, I was dressed entirely in black. My hair was hidden under the short, black veil of a postulant.

Moments later, I said goodbye as the heavy door closed behind them. I was completely shut away from the rest of the world. But despite all my youthful anticipation of a new life, my happiness faded quickly. By the second week I was already affected by being cut off from everything I had ever known. No matter how miserable life had been at home, my roots were there. My family was all I had. I began to cry every time I thought about them.

This was a semi-cloistered convent. So I lived each day isolated from the other nuns by a strict rule of silence, except for a few moments each evening. Soon a troubling loneliness engulfed me. Late into each night I paced the long, dark halls until I was worn out enough to shut out the emptiness in my heart and I could try to sleep.

Unquestioning obedience was also required of me in every detail of my life. I found this strict submission a constant, unsettling strain to comply with. Yet I submitted because this was what was rigidly required of me as a nun.

Although I was no longer glad to be there, I decided to stay because I was taught a new understanding of God. He was no longer my friend. Now I learned He was someone who wanted me to suffer so that I could fully do His will. The more I suffered, the more pleased He was with me.

So I tried to do everything I was told that God expected of me.

Yet I felt so troubled. The comfort and peace I used to find by being with God was gone. Now I only felt like I could never do enough to earn His approval.

After six months I became a novice. My name was changed to Sister Naomi and my hair was cropped short and hidden under a long, white veil. I gave myself wholeheartedly to living the life of a nun.

But no matter how hard I tried to do everything I was told to do, I constantly felt like I was drowning in sadness.

"God, please help me," I often prayed as I wearily knelt alone in the dark shadows of the chapel at night. "I feel so terribly alone and You are now so far away from me. You are the only one who has ever loved me and all I've ever wanted was to serve You. I'll do whatever You want me to do. But what are You asking of me?"

I yearned for an answer to that haunting question that tormented me. Night after night I watched the votive lights flickering in the dark shadows of the chapel while I quietly cried. But there was no answer. My private agony continued. All the help I used to receive from talking to God as a child was gone. I had a difficult time feeling close to someone who wanted me to hurt this much just so that I could do His will. I longed to find a place where I could be happy. But I was afraid to leave. I was now taught that if I left the convent, I would be turning my back on God and I couldn't stand the thought of living with such a terrible guilt.

After a year and a half I made public vows of poverty, chastity and obedience. The white veil was changed to a black one. I accepted my extreme unhappiness as the suffering I must endure to dedicate my life to God.

Meanwhile Pop's health deteriorated.

After he tried to kill himself he was forcibly committed to a state mental hospital. Ever since I entered the convent, Mother Superior refused to let me go see him. But finally she gave me permission to visit him one time.

Pop's eyes flickered with recognition as soon as I walked into his dimly lit room. I stood quietly by his bed while he lapsed in and out of consciousness. His gaunt face was ashen with the pallor of imminent death.

Yet despite his weakened condition, he was keenly aware that I was with him. He held on tight to my hand and wouldn't let it go. Tears streamed down my cheeks as the years with my father flashed before me. Ever since I left home, he tried to show me he loved me. He sent me encouraging letters, and handmade cards and incredible poems that he wrote about us and others that honored me as a person. In his own way, Pop tried his best to tell me he was sorry for hurting me.

While I stared at him, I reflected on the time I angrily told him I hated him. As stood there, I deeply regretted those cruel words and wanted so bad to say to him, "Pop, I didn't hate you. I'm so sorry I said that to you. I love you, Pop. I really do...."

But I left without speaking those words.

He died the next morning.

The wail of my sobs echoed down the long, dark corridor outside my room. I wept over the loss of a relationship that had never happened for us and now it was impossible. There was no place of comfort to run to because God was no longer someone I trusted with how I was honestly feeling.

In the weeks that followed Pop's death I longed to leave the convent. But that thought always tormented me with guilt. I also had no confidence I could make it out there on my own. Yet a year later I finally accepted that I couldn't live as a nun for the rest of my life. When the day of my departure finally arrived, I removed the black veil for the last time and dressed in the clothes my family brought for me.

"I wonder what the future will hold for me," I asked myself as I stared pensively into the full-length mirror. Gone was the girl of eighteen who was young, hopeful, and full of dreams of a happy new life. The woman I saw in the mirror was a stranger to me and the strict life of a cloistered nun was the only reality I had known since I was eighteen. Now I was twenty-two and I hardly recognized who I had become. But what was really scary is I had no understanding of the ways the world had dramatically changed while I had been hidden away all those. I sighed apprehensively, finished getting dressed and slowly descended the long flight of stairs that led to the front door. Several nuns waited to say goodbye.

"Are you absolutely sure, Sister Naomi that you have to leave us?" my favorite older nun asked as she held me in her arms and cried. "Yes, sister," I assured her. "I must go," and hurried out the door into the waiting car.

Convent Life Ends

"Maybe now that I'm older things will be different at home," I tried to convince myself during the long, silent ride back to where I used to live. "Maybe now we will be close."

But home wasn't different. My brothers and sisters were even more distant than when we were growing up. They had no room for me in their lives and my mother didn't want me around. Within days, the same loneliness returned that had been so troubling for me the years I was growing up.

I desperately needed a supportive place of safety to temporarily stay so that I could re-establish my life. Instead, I was forced to accept the harsh reality that I didn't have a home to come back to and no one I belonged to.

After I lived with Mom for only two weeks, she pressured me to move out and I had to face that I had no family and no one who cared if I was alright. I frantically looked for work and found a low paying job that I could get to by bus. With my first paycheck, I secured an inexpensive apartment that was far away from anyone in my family. I had no idea it was located in one of the most dangerous neighborhoods in Oakland, California.

I had given to God the best years of my youth, only to have my dream to serve Him crushed by disillusionment. After I had paid such a dear price to love Him, I felt He had betrayed me. I couldn't talk to Him. I wanted nothing to do with going to church. The song in my heart that I used to love to sing to Him died and my world was disturbing and dark. I forced myself to drink to escape the frightening chaos churning inside of me. I hated the taste of alcohol. But the only way I could block out the pain was to pass out drunk each night so that I could escape into sleep.

I immediately began to invite different men into my apartment to stay the night. All I could think about was I needed someone to love me.

That's when I met George, an older man who was charming and attentive. He quickly won my heart because he said all the words I always wanted someone to say to me.

We began to spend every possible moment together. He drank heavily, but I didn't give this any thought because I also was drinking way too much. But as soon as he moved into my apartment, our relationship changed. His flattering words ended and now he coldly rejected any of my efforts to be close to him.

"I miss the way we used to talk," I said to him early one summer evening as I lay beside him in bed. I hoped he would care that I was hurting. "Please talk to me," I pleaded. He rolled over in bed, turned his back to me and ignored me.

"You used to talk to me," I blurted out. "I don't understand what's happening between us."

I became even more agitated as I angrily glared at him lying there, ignoring me in an icy silence. With no warning, George leaped out of bed and pinned me against the wall. I was stunned as his large hand came at me. I frantically covered my face and head with my arms as he punched me over and over. My head wrenched from side to side with each forceful blow.

"Stop!" I screamed hysterically. "Please stop!"

He ignored my frightened pleas. Then just as suddenly as his rage had begun, it ended. I slumped to the floor and my bruised body went limp. I gasped for air as he walked away from me and sullenly went back to bed.

After that night, I couldn't relax whenever I was around him.

Yet I still married him.

After our marriage, George kept a loaded gun in a nightstand by our bed and every time I hid it, he found it and put it back in the drawer. One afternoon he aimed that gun at me and yelled loud threats that he was going to kill me.

That was the beginning of living each day anxiously wondering when he would actually kill me.

I began drinking early in the morning to muster up the strength to face each day. Soon I added drugs in a futile attempt to block out even more of my pain. To hide my husband's abuse, I didn't let people get close to me. I was too ashamed to let anyone find out what was really going on in our home. That withdrawal isolated me from anyone who could have helped me.

While I slipped deeper and deeper into a suicidal despair, I gave birth to a daughter. A year and a half later my son was born. But I hated my husband. I despised who I had become. I constantly saw how I was failing my two young children and guilt haunted me. I hated Mom. Disturbing memories of how she had hurt me battered my emotions and exhausted me. Day and night, I relived each scarring, horrible incident. There was no escape from my overwhelming distress.

God Comes

One bleak afternoon I wearily stared out of the second story window of our shabby, dimly lit apartment.

The dark winter sky cast an ominous gray pallor over the deserted street below.

I was only thirty years old, but I had no hope to look forward to. I felt frighteningly alone and no amount of alcohol or drugs could silence my desperation.

As I walked over to the window and pressed my forehead against the cold glass, I couldn't contain the explosive emotions now convulsing on the inside of me. All I could think about was how to kill myself. I hadn't talked to God in many years. But I had no one else to turn to as I buckled over in pain and hid my face in my trembling hands.

"Oh God," I sobbed. "I used to be so close to You when I was a little girl. You were all I had and I don't even know when I lost You. But, I desperately need You now. I beg You to be real to me again. If You don't help me, I don't want to live any longer. I feel too lost. I'm too scared. Please help me."

His presence filled the room.

It was the same comforting closeness I knew as a child. I stood there in hushed awe as I hungrily soaked up that He came to be with me and to help me.

"Ruth, I hear your cries," I sensed He was trying to tell me. I'm right here and I'm going to help you. I've wanted to help you all along. I've just been waiting for you to want to be close to Me again."

"Lord," I whispered. "It's You. It's really You. It's been such a long, long time since I've felt close to You. I thought I had lost You forever. I've missed You so much."

Then with the same kindness I remembered when He used to be My Friend, He promised me, "I'm going to show you where to find Me. You are going to be alright."

Just as suddenly as He had come, His presence left. Yet hope had been stirred up within me.
I decided I wouldn't rest until I found Him again. So I began to visit different churches of many denominations looking for His presence.

Six months went by and the search was becoming disheartening.

Finally one Sunday morning I walked into a small church while the pastor was preaching on the story of Naomi and Ruth.

"God loved Ruth," he explained in a kind voice as I sat down in a wooden pew at the back of the church. "He wanted to protect Naomi. He wanted to take care of her every need."

"Oh Lord," I silently prayed as tears streamed down my face. "No one here knows me. This pastor has no idea that my name is Ruth. He doesn't know that my name in the convent was Sister Naomi. Only You know this. You gave him this sermon for me. You care about me that much. You really do!"

This amazing love filled my weary heart.

At the end of the service, when the pastor asked if anyone wanted to be saved, I went quickly to the altar and told Jesus, "I open myself up to You completely. I give everything I am to You and I want all You have for me."

I stayed there a long time as a healing peace flooded my soul.

For the first time in my life I felt myself relax and terrible loneliness that had preyed on my mind since I was a little girl was gone. The presence of God that I had searched for was with me again.

All I had ever wanted was to have someone love me and now I was restored to the only Person who had ever given me that love.

During those radically life-changing moments, the dream that God birthed in my heart at the age of six suddenly came back to life with a renewed passion to serve Him with all that I am.

I once again began to sing to Him with my own, simple songs of love as an overwhelming gratitude bubbled up out of my spirit and washed over me like a refreshing river.

"Lord," I told Him. "I never want this song to die again."

The Reign of Terror Ends

I had high hopes that getting saved would begin the healing in my marriage.

Instead, George despised my love for Jesus and His cruelty and violent outbursts of rage escalated. I became increasingly more frightened for the safety of myself and the children.

One Saturday morning toward the end of my first year as a Christian, our vulnerably young son and daughter sat at the kitchen table in tense silence and listened to us argue.

Without any warning, he lunged at me, furiously wrapped his hands around my neck, and dragged me across the kitchen floor.

"I'm going to kill you!" he screamed as he brutally squeezed my neck tighter and tighter.

My arms thrashed uncontrollably. I panicked and gasped for air. In a futile effort to wrench free from his grip, I grabbed at his hands. Suddenly I went limp in his grasp. I was too petrified to fight back. I could only beg him to stop with my terrified eyes. Seconds later George threw me to the floor. With his hands clenched in tight fists at his side, he stormed out of the room.

The children crept quietly away from the kitchen table and ran to their rooms, too scared to speak or even look at me. For the remainder of that weekend I lived every second with a paralyzing fear.

"What if he turns on me again?" I kept saying in a panic to myself. "What if he attacks one of the children? What if I say the wrong thing and he tries to strangle me again? The next time he might actually kill me!"

I tensely waited for an opportunity to escape with my children and I left him.

But I foolishly thought I had ended my problem.

Consequently, after just a few months when I met Dan at church, I was drawn to him like he was a giant magnet.

Six months later we were married.

I was horrified to discover on our honeymoon that he also was cruel. Then rapidly he became far more destructively abusive than I had ever experienced.

I pleaded with God to help me and what He began to show me is captured in the rest of this book. Each revelation radically changed me and this quote captures why:

"God didn't reveal Himself to us in a theology textbook.

Instead He wrote a love story. We call it the Bible." *Andrew Peters*

Chapter Three

WE NEED A DAD

I lost many years going from one destructive relationship to another. I was searching for someone to love me so that the shattered places in my heart could stop hurting.

But none of these efforts ever worked. They always ended in heartbreaking loss that made the pain worse.

Only when I let God become my very real Dad did this emotional torment stop and I had the courage to put behind me the grief I had felt since I was a little girl.

I eventually became so whole that it was as if none of the agony of my past mattered anymore. All the sad memories of overwhelming rejection from mom and pop stopped dominating my thoughts. They no longer controlled my choices.

None of this was easy to do.

It meant I had to make a lot of constant, hard choices. But my transformation did happen.

The nightmare of my past did end.

What made all this possible was me getting to know God more and more as the first real Dad I had ever known.

His understanding love as my Father gave me the courage to keep on making more and more healthy choices that were nothing like the way I used to be.

What also changed me was experiencing in many difficult situations that He was never too busy to be there for me whenever I needed a Father's encouragement and support.

He never condemned me, no matter how much I "blew it." He did let me know whenever I was going the wrong direction. But then with a lot of kindness He helped me find my way back to where I could be at peace again.

For those who have never experienced this amazing love of the Father, it's one of the main reasons you are hurting with sadness and emptiness in your soul.

It's also why life can feel scary, overwhelming and confusing at times. Not having a father who loved us when we were young can cause all this because God gives us an earthly dad to be a steadying source of wisdom and love during the hard times as we try to find our way in life.

We especially need this fatherly support when we begin young adulthood and there are so many new challenges that can get really confusing, even troubling to figure out by ourselves.

Yet if we missed out on getting that help from our earthly dad, worse yet if we were hurt by our dad growing up, we may not want anything to do with God as a Father.

I certainly didn't want it when I began my life as a Christian. This was my "not so great" attitude when I was saved:

"Jesus is my Savior and I love Him.

But I want nothing to do with God as my Father.

That I have no interest in at all."

Those were tragic years in my life when the word "father" was one of the ugliest words in the English language.

I also had no clue that this rejection deeply saddened Jesus because the Father meant everything to Him.

I was so sorry when I realized this. That's when I decided to let God have a chance to be that close to me.

It's also when I experienced a comfort I'd never known before as His kindness began to melt the walls around my heart. It was the beginning of Him becoming the first **real** Father I'd ever known.

What helped to have a breakthrough is realizing that when we give Him a chance to have this kind of relationship with us, we are able to discover that He can be the most supportive Dad we could ever hope for and a caring Father who can always be depended on to keep this promise

**"I will never leave you.
I will never abandon you."**
Hebrews 13:5 NLT

The Word also reveals this amazing insight into who God is:

> "You have not received a spirit of slavery leading to fear again. You have received a spirit of adoption, by which you may cry out to Me, 'Abba Father.'"
>
> Romans 8:15 NASB

I was actually surprised when I learned that the Greek for "Abba Father" is as personal and intimate a name as if we were saying "Papa God" or "dear Daddy."

This very personal relationship with God is what you and I need because He ***does*** have a "plan for us, for good and not destruction, to give us a future and a hope." Yet we are seriously limited in being able to enter into all that He has for us if we feel sad and empty inside because we don't have Him as our Dad to help us.

**This is what I discovered about God
that completely changed how I looked at Him.**

He is a Father who Cares

He is not oblivious to what we are going through.

God is the Creator of all. But He has the same concern for our welfare that any loving earthly father has toward his child.

He also wants us to have such an unwavering confidence in His love that we are able to say with absolute certainty:

"God is just like a real Dad. He will find a way to help me, no matter what."

His Word assures us that this is definitely how He feels about us:

"I have cared about you, again and again, in your time of wilderness, just as a father cares for his child.

Whenever you cry out, 'I am slipping.' My unfailing love will support you. You will not be shaken because I am right by your side.

Do not be afraid or discouraged. I go before you. I am with you wherever you go.

When you go through deep waters and great trouble, I will be with you.

When you go through rivers of difficulty, you will not drown.

You can say to yourself, with confidence 'My Father is my helper.

I will not be afraid.'"

Joshua 1:9, Isaiah 43:2 NLT, Hebrews 13:6 NASB
Deuteronomy 1:31, Psalm 94:18, 16:8 NLT

He's a Dad who inspires us to believe we have a Purpose

A father's affirmation births a sense of destiny in the heart of a child. That's why without his encouragement, hope can die in us at a young age.

The Father compassionately understands how much this loss hurts us. He longs for us to know that He believes in all we can ever possibly become and what's really powerful is that our destiny comes from Him. So all the days of our life He will do all He can to help us fulfill His purpose for us. These are the verses that helped me understand how much this is the Father's heart:

> "I know the plans I have for you, plans to prosper you and not to harm you, plans to give you hope and a future. So be glad for all I am planning for you. For I will keep on guiding you with My counsel. I will lead you to a glorious destiny."
>
> Romans 12:12 NLT
> Jeremiah 29:11 NIV
> Psalm 73:23 NLT

He restores the Lost Years

I grew up feeling a deep sense of loss because my father was never there for me when I needed a dad. My hopes to share my life with him always ended in devastating disappointment.

Then because I felt I wasn't good enough to be acceptable to Pop, I wasn't comfortable anywhere I went. I didn't seem to fit in. I never felt that I belonged. This lack of relationship with a father can be the result of him not being in a child's life at all or it can come from having a dad who was physically present, but distant emotionally. Both kinds of rejection leave scars that make it extremely difficult to establish healthy relationships as an adult. Consequently, the sense of loss can get far more painful as the years go by.

But God doesn't want us to spend the rest of our life being affected by not having an earthly dad who loved us.

He earnestly longs to make it up to us for what we missed out on, through no fault of our own.

He's also the only one who can set us free from this crushing emotional pain and what's monumentally encouraging is that He *can* do all this because He's a Dad who means it when He tells us:

"My child,

I sent My Son to set you free so that you could become My very own child.

My unchanging plan has always been to adopt you into My own family by bringing you to Myself through My Son, Jesus. So now you are My very own child and you can call Me 'Father, dear Father.'

If you've never had a father, I really want to be that Dad to you because I am a Father to the fatherless. I long for you to know that even if your earthly father was not there for you, I won't ever abandon you. I only want to take care of you and hold you close as My loved child.

So please be comforted.

I'm here to transform your Valley of Trouble into a Gateway of Hope so that I can restore your soul and give you back what you lost.

I even want to renew your youth like the eagle and turn into good everything that the enemy has ever meant for evil against you.

For as your Dad I am here to open refreshing rivers in the midst of your valleys. I can even show you the path to My peace so that you can leave behind you your deep discouragement and never go back to that barren desert ever again.

- Your Father who loves you and cares about you as a Dad who loves you with all My Heart"

Psalms 27:10, 68:5-6, 16:8, 9:10 NLT/NASB/MOFFATT
Galatians 4:5-6, Romans 5:15, 8:15 NLT/NASB
Hebrews 13:5, Ephesians 1:5-6 NLT/KJV
Jeremiah 3:19, 1 John 3:1 NLT

Isaiah 40:1-2 NLT, Hosea 2:15 NLT
Ezekiel 36:11, Genesis 50:20 NLT

Joel 2:25, Jeremiah 31:4 NLT
Isaiah 41:18, 43:19, 51:3 NASB
Psalm 23:3, 103:5 NASB
Psalm 84:6 NLT

As I saw all these amazing insights into how God feels about us, I realized I no longer needed to feel like an outsider as I went through life. I was not a misfit or unacceptable.

This very new way of how I saw myself made it possible for me to start learning how to enjoy being me. I also no longer felt empty inside.

As a result of these huge changes, the unhealthy people I used to be drawn to for personal relationship I was no longer attracted to and the kinds of destructive, abusive, unhealthy people who use to like me a lot now were not interested in knowing me at all.

Oh my!

I had such fun celebrating these radical changes.

Each one affected me in an incredibly positive way and in every area of my life.

The Father holds our Hand

There is nothing more comforting to a young child than walking by his father's side with his little hand in his dad's big, strong hand.

I vividly remember the day when I ached to experience that reassuring closeness.

This is that story.

"Would you like to go to the park with me today?" Pop asked my sister and me early one morning when I was nine years old.

"Sure!" we told him excitedly. With happy anticipation we walked by his side to the bus stop. Soon we boarded the bus that took us far from our home to a place I had never been.

"I have to go somewhere for just a few minutes," Pop told us. "I promise I'll be right back."

I watched heavyhearted as he walked away from us down the street. But eventually I reluctantly sat on the grass while my sister wandered off to play by herself. I just kept anxiously waiting for Pop to return. Not far from where I was sitting, a young girl and her father came into view. She walked by his side while he held her hand. As I watched longingly, her dad picked her up and held her close to him on his shoulder.

"I wish I had a father like that," I said wistfully to myself. I wish Pop were here and he would hold me like that so that I could feel safe and not hurt anymore."

After a while I grew weary of waiting and walked around the park. But I couldn't enjoy being there.

I kept hoping that at any moment I would see my father coming toward me. Night came and I was very hungry. I shivered from the cold while I watched a group of children having a birthday party in a large picnic area. As soon as they left, I frantically rummaged through the garbage pail by their table for leftover food and ate whatever I could find. Much later Pop arrived.

"Sorry I took so long," he mumbled apologetically.

"Where were you," I asked as I tried my very best to hold back my tears. "I waited so long for you."

"I got tied up," was all he replied.

My sister and I sat in silence next to him all the way home. Tears rolled down my cheeks while I stared out into the darkness of the night. I felt so lost, so alone, so overwhelmingly sad. Waves of pain crushed my heart that already felt so fragile.

The wound from this incident went deep into my soul. The devastating feelings of rejection stayed in the troubled recesses of my heart and nothing could silence them.

Yet there came a day when this sadness no longer had the power to poison my soul. All torment was gone any time I thought about that day in the park.

That astounding change took place when I discovered that God is a kind Dad who always wants to hold me by the hand.

As this surprising revelation became a part of me, I began to feel secure in ways I had never experienced before.

This is when I realized that every time we are afraid, all we have to do is cry out, "Father! I'm scared! Please take my hand and help me."

Then peace can return to our soul as He gently, compassionately reassures us:

"Everything's going to be alright."

These are the scriptures that inspired this phenomenal breakthrough:

"I will hold you by the hand and watch over you.

I am the Lord, your God, who takes hold of your right hand and says to you, 'Do not be afraid. I will help you.'

And whenever you fall down you will not be hurled headlong, for I am the one who is holding you by the hand."
Psalm 37:24, Isaiah 41:13, 42:6 NASB

The Father Carries us

When life gets too hard for a young child, he needs to have his earthly father pick him up and carry him.

This caring intervention helps him relax inside.

It gives him the confidence that he can make it.

The problem is that once we grow up, no one can meet this need except the Father.

If we look for this security and fatherly comfort from others, we are wide open to being attracted to abusive relationships that will only make the pain in vulnerable places in our heart far more devastating.

But the awesome good news is that God *can* meet this need. In these tender, kind words He expresses that this is His heart toward us:

"My child,

All the days of your life, I long to pick you up and hold you close to Me when life is too difficult. I want to do this for you in the same way a loving father carries his own son or daughter.

- Your Father who is here for you any time you need a Dad's help"

Deuteronomy 1:31 NASB, Isaiah 63:9, 40:11
Psalm 68:19 NLT

God hurts when we Hurt

Nothing causes a loving earthly father more heartache than to know that his child is hurting.

God feels this same way.

Whenever we were in pain as a child, He saw what was happening to us. He grieved every time we were abused.

It broke His heart that the parents He gave us would choose to do terrible things to us. In all our suffering,

He longed to reach down and scoop us up into His arms so that He could compassionately help us to feel cared about and safe.

But He had to wait until we were willing to give Him a chance to be our Dad.

Only then could He pour His healing love into our broken heart.

This is what the Father is saying to anyone who is suffering because of pain from their childhood.

"My child,

Cry out to Me and I will hear you. I will answer you and I will show you the way to wholeness and freedom.

I'm always here for you, with arms open wide because I long to help you.

I ache for your suffering to end and for you to find a refuge in the safe shelter of My understanding compassion for all you have suffered.

I have seen your troubles and I want you to know that I care deeply about the anguish of your soul.

I care so much about you that whenever you were hurt, I grieved and felt your horrible pain   .

Please hear My heart that when life is hard on you, and whenever you are suffering, I long to draw you close to Me. I yearn to shelter you beneath the shadow of My wings until each storm you are up against is past. Oh how I want to still the waves and bring you safely into harbor. How I ache for you to feel reassured that no matter what, I will never, ever push you away when you need Me to be there for you as your safe harbor and your Dad.

- Your Father who cares about you more than you could possibly ever imagine"

Psalm 68:6, 124:7, 118:5 NLT/NASB
Isaiah 44:22, 49:9 NLT

God is a Dad who is never Harsh

If we had an earthly father who expected too much of us, we learned to be too hard on ourselves. We grew up feeling like a failure because it was impossible for us to live up to his expectations. Eventually we decided it isn't worth trying or we went to the other extreme and constantly tried to excel. In that case, we could never completely relax inside due to all the pressure we put on our self to achieve and try to be perfect. We were driven to do whatever it took to earn our father's approval.

My adult daughter, Mary, shares a sad example of what all this feels like. Her story makes God's heart ache for *every* child who has ever suffered in this way:

"From as early as I can remember, I felt defeated by my dad expecting too much from me.

I remember when I was nine years old. I clutched my report card proudly in my hand all the way home from the last day of school.

As our house came into view at the end of the street, I told myself, 'I can hardly wait to show Dad my grades. I know he'll be so proud of me for getting all A's and just one B.' The B was in math. I hated math.

But I had worked my very best all year long to earn a good grade in it.

So I was especially excited to show him that B.

'Look, Dad,' I told him with a beaming smile as soon as he walked through the front door later that afternoon. 'Look at my report card. I did real good. I know you'll be very proud of me.'

I happily handed it to him. But my smile quickly faded. I anxiously watched as he examined it in stony silence and with a serious expression on his face.

'What's this B all about?' he blurted out in a harsh, disapproving voice. 'You could have done better than that in math if you had tried harder.'

'But I did try hard, Dad. I tried my very best. And the A's. Aren't you happy...?'

I didn't get to finish what I was saying before he interrupted me.

'The B is not good enough, he harshly told me. 'I expect an A in math next time,' as if I hadn't accomplished anything at all. Then he handed the report card back to me and walked away. Crushed by his disappointment in me, I ran into my room, threw myself on the bed and buried my face in the pillow to muffle my sobs.

'I'll just have to try harder,' I told myself as I cried with such a broken heart. 'That's all I can do. Somehow I'll have to try harder.' I was too young to understand that my father's expectations were impossible to live up to. So I blamed myself for never being good enough.

That scenario occurred every time I brought a report card home from school.

By the time I got to junior high, I didn't care anymore. I just gave up. I knew that no matter how much I tried to please my dad, my very best efforts would never be good enough for him.

'So why bother trying,' I eventually concluded."

Mary never recovered from the damage that the abusive expectation did to her. She was meant to be so happy and had so many remarkable ways she could have succeeded in life.

It was tragic to watch her completely give up and be drowned in despair while only a teenager.

Yet my hope and prayer is that some day she will find her way to being fully healed and restored. I long to have this happen for Mary and I know that God will do all He can to help her find her way there. He will never give up on trying to help her.

Being absolutely secure in knowing that He is this kind of Father is how I find comfort whenever I think of how much my daughter is still in such tremendous pain.

But for all who have been hurt as she has been, I'm grateful that God isn't a stern taskmaster who closely watches us so that He can criticize us the minute we make a mistake.

He doesn't demand perfection.

He won't crush us with discouraging expectations that we can never live up to.

Rather He's a Dad who looks past our flaws and even all our failures and sees our heart.

He then aches to pour His reassurance into our heart so that we have the confidence to face the difficult challenges of life and not give up.

This is what He did for Peter after he betrayed Jesus by publicly denying he even knew Him. Yet when Peter was sorry and heartbroken over what he had done to his Best Friend, he then went on to be a highly honored and powerfully used leader in the birth of the church.

The Father does all this when we have a humble, repentant heart.

He also understands our tremendous need to be encouraged so that we have the courage to keep on trying, rather than caving into despair when we fail.

In these kind words He assures us that this is how He feels:

"My dearly loved child,

Just as a father has compassion on his child, I have compassion on you. I made your heart, so I always understand how you are feeling. When you are having a hard time, I actually bend down and listen to you.

So please, give all your worries and cares to Me. I care more about each of them more than you could ever know. Each time you talk to Me about all that is in your heart that hurts so much, I promise you I will encourage you. I will give you the strength you need to not give up.

I also assure you that I understand the hopes of the helpless.

So I will always listen to your cries and comfort you. Just as a kind shepherd tenderly holds a fragile, vulnerable lamb close to his heart, every moment of your life I am here to hold you that close to Me.

I am here, no matter what, to help you have the courage to live life to the fullest.

All of your life, since the moment you were born, I have longed and ached to be able to help you find your way to that courage and enter I into all I have planned for you.

- Your Father who loves you and tenderly cares about you every moment of your life"

Psalm 116:2, 33:15, 10:17, 103:13-14, 138:3 NLT/NASB
1 Chronicles 28:9, Isaiah 40:11 NLT
I Peter 5:7 NLT

God corrects, but only with Love

If our earthly father abused us when he corrected us, we learned to fear his harsh discipline. We dreaded being around him when we made a mistake. If this is how we grew up, we never experienced that a caring earthly father corrects his child out of love and not with a cruel disregard for his child's feelings.

What my daughter shares illustrates the damage those feelings inflict on a child.

"I always felt growing up that my father's motivation for disciplining me was to control my opinions and feelings.

No matter what I talked to him about, he was always right and I was always wrong. What I had to say or how I felt was never valid to him.

If I didn't immediately agree with him, he grabbed me, hit me or said cruel words to me. He demanded my respect, but he never treated me with respect and he never tried to understand me.

'You are the child and I am the parent,' I remember him telling me whenever I objected to him being mean or degrading toward me. 'God doesn't tell me to respect you, but He commands you to respect me,' he always insisted.

By the time I went into junior high, I felt that no one wanted to understand me. I turned my anger toward anyone in authority who came down hard on me.

I rebelled if I ever thought an adult was making a judgment about me without listening to my opinions or feelings. I couldn't handle it if someone didn't treat me with respect."

The suffering my daughter experienced is repeated in the life of any child whose father abuses him through harsh discipline. But God is a very different kind of Father. He wants the best for us. That's the only reason He ever corrects us.

He never beats us over the head with His Word. His correction doesn't destroy us or frighten us. He never tries to control us. His presence in our life as a Dad never causes us to feel degraded or abused.

He only encourages us to seek Him and be close to Him so that He can help us have the wisdom to make the right choices. He does this so that He can bless our life. He warns us when we are going in the wrong direction. But only to protect us from doing the things that will end up hurting us.

As a caring Father, He only wants to help us have a happy life.

Our caring Father will not Hurt us

When a child grows up with abuse from a dad, the word "father" becomes an ugly word. The very mention of it stirs up the painful thought:

"If that's what having a dad feels like, I don't need it."

It breaks God's heart when this happens to those who are young and innocent because then they don't want to know Him. Nonetheless, this is His heart toward those who have been abused by their earthly father and as a result they are not open to a relationship with Him:

"I never want to hurt you.

I only want to rescue you so that you will no longer be abused and destroyed."
Lamentations 3:33 NLT
Ezekiel 34:22 NLT

This story illustrates how a father's abuse can turn a young person away from God and destroy any desire for a relationship with Him.

My son was seventeen when Dave, one of his best friends was killed in a car accident. He was a straight "A" student who was active in the youth group in his church and was a strong Christian. My son admired him immensely. Dave was what he would call "a really good kid." Many of his other friends ditched school and partied. Dave was the one who always stayed out of trouble and tried to do the right thing.

One day the phone rang. My son was shocked by what the voice on the other end of the line was telling him. "He's dead. Dave's dead," his friend told him.

He hung up the phone and sat down in a chair across from his father. He was shaken and stunned.

"Why Dave, dad?" he said in a loud, hurt voice. "Why did God let him die? He was such a good person and such a good Christian. Why did God let this happen? If anybody deserved to die, it's me or all my other loser friends who are always pulling stuff. I hate God for doing this. I hate Him for letting Dave die."

Without any warning, his father jumped up out of his chair and lunged at him. He was a tall, solidly built man and with all his strength he slugged him in the face.

"You don't talk about God like that," he told this hurting teenager with a religious, self-righteous indignation.

When my son poured out his pain, he needed his dad to understand his overwhelming grief and confusion. He needed compassion, not an abusive slug in his face.

Sadly, he was never the same about Christianity after that incident. He already had been struggling with how he felt about it because of all the times his father had used the Bible to condemn him. After that brutal experience, he understandably wanted nothing to do with the God his dad believed in.

I'm so thankful this isn't the end of the story.

My son grew into a wonderful man with a passion for life. He's an amazing, inspiring person who refused to let his past destroy him.

Despite all he suffered, he has a special heart that is healthy and not bitter. He has pursued his hopes and dreams and his excellence of character gave him favor in his career.

I'm daily grateful for the remarkable person he's chosen to become. Yet my prayer for years has been that some day he will give God another chance. I long for him to experience the kind Father He really is, and that when his dad hit him it **wasn't** what God wanted **at all.**

Rather the Father hurt for him when his friend died and He fully understood my son's outburst of overwhelming pain and grief. He only wanted his dad to be kind and understanding to him and comfort him.

God is a Dad who longs to Heal us

Sometimes the hurts from an earthly father don't come from physical "blows."

Verbal and emotional abuse is actually quite often the hardest to ever overcome. My daughter, Mary tells her story that graphically captures the accuracy of this insight.

"When I was thirteen years old, I was arrested for stealing candy from the convenience store across the street from junior high school. Mom had to pick me up at the police station. I knew she was upset and I felt bad that I had hurt her.

But dad was the one I dreaded seeing.

By this time he already had a history of being abusive toward me and I was scared he would beat me up for this incident.

I sat tensely on the living room couch, anxiously waiting for him to come home from work and as soon as I heard his car in the driveway, I panicked.

'Look at what you've done now!' he screamed at me as he stormed into the room and stopped angrily in front of me. He towered over where I sat on the couch and glared at me. His face was contorted with the revulsion he felt toward me.

'I....'

Before I could finish he spit in my face. Instant rage welled up inside me as I wiped his spit away with my sleeve.

'You have no right to do that to me!' I screamed at him. 'You have no right!'

'You're a loser!' he yelled back at me. 'That's what you are. A loser! I have every right to treat you any way I want. You got exactly what you deserve. God is just as disgusted with you as I am."

He then quoted scriptures to prove how much God supported him treating me this way.

I frantically ran out of the room and into my bedroom while he shouted at me, 'You get back here right this minute. I'm not finished with you yet!'

I slammed the door behind me and slumped to the floor by my bed and sobbed hysterically. I was relieved that he didn't come after me and force me to go back into the living room.

'I feel like scum under his feet,' I told myself as I buried my face in my trembling hands as I rocked back and forth, trying to stop crying and get over the degrading shock of what had just happened.

'I'm nothing to my father but a piece of dirt,' I told myself.

At that moment I wanted to die. I would rather he had taken a knife and killed me than live with how degraded I felt from his spit that I could still feel on my face. From that day I wanted to hurt my dad as much as he had hurt me. I also tried many times to kill myself. I remember thinking a lot, 'If I have to hurt like this all of the time, what's the point of living?'"

Mary had witnessed her biological father's violence toward me as a young child. When I remarried, the cruelty from this second father now crushed her even more. Anger and hatred consumed her. She turned to drugs to desperately try to stop her pain.

In her late teens, she lived with different older men who used and mistreated her. They always ended up discarding her as if she were a worthless piece of trash.

Eventually she lived on the streets of the town where she grew up, deeply troubled and lost. No matter how much I wished it were possible, I couldn't change the past or erase all her suffering. I couldn't undo the damage.

I could only keep showing her how much I loved her and pray that someday God would make it up to her for the years that had been destroyed in her life.

While I carried all this in my heart, He did often warn me to pray for her safety. Then days later she inevitably appeared at my doorstep.

Underneath the heavy makeup and hardened countenance, I saw a frightened little girl who was desperate to know that she still had family who loved her.

"You were praying for me the other night, Mom," she would say with a haunted look in her eyes. "I know you were praying. It's your prayers that protected me. I would have been killed, Mom, if you hadn't been praying."

Then just as quickly as she had come, she walked away and disappeared down the street. I ached for her.

All I could do was trust God to protect her until she found her way back to Him and when Mary was twenty-six years old, He answered my prayers. She became so scared by what was happening in her life that she decided to enter Teen Challenge. She gave her life back to Jesus and eventually returned home. Our friendship helped to heal her regrets for all the years we missed out on as mother and daughter. She found a job, enrolled in college and immediately excelled in both.

But as she grew older, the wounds from all the degrading treatment by her father overwhelmed her and in heartrending ways eventually destroyed her.

Yet even though her life is full of so much horribly crushing loss, she often talks about how much she depends on God to help her keep going.

She knows He is real and that He cares about her. She also realizes that He feels only compassion for all she has suffered because of the abuse from her dad. For all this I am deeply grateful.

But how my heart aches for all the sons and daughters who don't want to give God a chance to be their Dad because of hurts they suffered from their earthly father.

This book was actually birthed from that place of longing and ache for those who need help finding their way to wholeness and peace.

There is another disturbing way that an earthly father can overpower a child with abuse that desperately needs to be healed by the Father. It comes from a dad leaning on his son or daughter for his emotional or sexual needs. These scars go deep. Troubled, confused feelings come into the heart of that child because the parent he was supposed to be able to trust ended up violating him.

My brother's story is a tragic example of the damage this betrayal inflicts on an innocent, trusting child.

When Joe was born I was nine years old. As soon as he came home from the hospital, he was left alone in his crib most of the time. I couldn't stand to see him lying there with no one caring about him. So I tried as hard as I could to give him the love he was missing.

But I could never give him enough affection to make up for Mom's neglect.

As Joe got older, my father developed an unhealthy bond with him. The more distant Pop's relationship was with my mother, the more he turned to my brother for his need for companionship.

Joe was also starved for love. So they grew increasingly more dependent on each other in a sick, destructive way. Each day they spent many hours alone together. Pop found in Joe a way to meet his sexual and emotional needs. This changed my brother into a deeply disturbed young boy.

When he was in late grammar school, Pop's health deteriorated. He leaned more and more on my brother. This was a heavy burden for such a young child.

As a result, Joe felt way too responsible to be there for his father. He rarely went outside to play and was robbed of many of the experiences a boy his age needs to enjoy.

"Could you stay home with me?" my father asked Joe early one morning just before he walked out the door to go to school. "I don't want to be alone today. I really need you to be with me."

Joe struggled. He was visibly torn. There was a party at school that day and he didn't want to miss out on it.

But he also didn't want to let Pop down.

"No," Joe finally said as he hung his head down guiltily. "I really want to go to school. My teacher is doing something special with us today. We're having a party and I want to be there."

With those words, my brother shrugged his shoulders and left.

Pop died a few days after that and my brother never forgave himself for not staying home with him. Guilt tormented him. When he started high school, he tried to escape from his unbearable pain by getting into drugs and heavy drinking. He failed all his classes and one day, in a fit of rage, he attacked Mom. She called the police and they took him away. From that point, my brother deteriorated rapidly.

By the time he was eighteen, he was in and out of mental hospitals.

"I can't get over that I let Pop down," he always sadly told me whenever I visited him. "I can't get it out of my mind that I left him when he needed me just before he died."

I grieved over the tragic direction of his life.

But no matter how much I hurt for my brother, I couldn't help him. Slowly I watched the brother I loved with my very life become someone I no longer knew.

He was alive physically, but the real Joe had already died. He never came back to the person he was before Pop died.

If a parent violates his son or daughter by using him to meet his sexual or emotional needs like happened to my brother, that little girl or young boy may not end up as disturbed as he did. Nonetheless, the scars that are inflicted will leave any child disturbed and scarred in vulnerable places in their soul.

The only one who can set a soul free from such horrible pain is our merciful Father. He fully understands our shame and guilt. He feels compassion for how much we are suffering and longs to take all the troubled feelings out of us and give us a new heart.

He did all this for me and that is what gave me another chance at life. Therefore, I have personally experienced that the Father really does mean it when He says in these compelling words that He wants to give us His merciful, healing love:

"My child,

Please cry out to Me and I will heal the places in your heart where you feel terrible pain. I long to help you. I ache for you to know how much My heart grieved every time you were betrayed by someone you trusted and it should have been safe for you to let them be close to you.

I promise you, if you will give Me a chance, I will set you free. I will show you the way out of the torment of your past so that the heartbreaking damage can finally end and you can get on with the encouraging, fulfilling life I have planned for you to experience. With the deepest kind of compassion for all you have been through, I long to do all this for you.

- Your Father who is hurting for you and wants to love you as a Dad you can trust to love and be close to"

Psalm 30:2, 119:32 NLT/NIV
Isaiah 30:26, Ezekiel 36:36 NASB
Jeremiah 30:17 NASB

The Father Protects us

Every child has a serious need to know that his dad cares that he is safe. But if we grew up without feeling that our earthly father felt this way about us, we can spend the rest of our life looking for someone to give us that sense of security.

For me, a lifetime of feeling unsafe began after this incident happened in late grammar school.

We lived in the Projects.

It was a dangerous place. Crime, violence, screams and screeching sirens were a way of life for me.

My bedroom was an old kitchen with a bed in it and a door that led directly to the outside. Late one night I heard the footsteps of someone running. The steps came closer and closer. A fist smashed the glass panel of my door. It shattered. A man's gloved hand groped through the opening. I watched in horror as his fingers fumbled for the lock.

I wanted to scream, but I was too frightened to make a sound.

"In another moment," I told myself hysterically, "he's going to be in my room."

"Help! Help!" I finally yelled out in a piercing scream.

My family rushed into the room.

The man ran away and disappeared into the darkness outside.

"What's going on?" Pop mumbled sleepily from his bed at the other end of the house.

They told him what had happened. But he never got out of bed to make sure I was alright.

After everyone left, I wondered if that man would come back to hurt me. For the longest time, I lay trembling under my blankets, too afraid to move.

That was the night when the haunting nightmares of a man trying to kill me began.

Fear consumed me. It controlled my every waking moment and terrorized me whenever I tried to sleep.

As I grew older I wanted a man to come along and help me feel safe. But I learned the hard way this was a serious mistake because anyone we get involved with who is willing to be overly protective of us so that we can feel safe is a very unhealthy person.

Eventually the behaviors that we thought were helping us to feel secure can swiftly become a sick, stifling, oppressive, control.

The Father is the only one who can fill this painful void in our heart as an adult. And what's comforting is He is the kind of protective Dad we've longed for who **can** do this for us, and He passionately **wants** to.

It was through His Word that He helped me to see that we can run to Him whenever we are afraid and His sheltering presence will come to calm our worst fears.

I discovered He even hovers over us as we sleep so that we can close our eyes and peacefully rest in the safety of His kind, caring presence.

These are His amazing words that awakened my understanding to all this and set my heart free:

"My child,

I am your safe haven.

I am your Dad who longs for you experience how much I can be your safe haven, your hiding place, and your comforting refuge.

During any of your times of trouble and distress, you can rely on My protection, no matter how late it is at night or how early it is in the morning.

I never get tired. I never go to sleep.

I'm always here for you, wanting you to know I am protecting you and caring about you.

- Your Father who wants to reassure you so that you can feel completely safe"

Psalm 3:3, 43:2, 32:7,9:9, 68:2, 124:4, 5:12 NLT/NASB
2 Samuel 22:33 NLT, Isaiah 27:3-5 NASB
Deuteronomy 33:27 NLT

Because of this really new way of looking at God, I was no longer a frightened little girl inside.

Stability came into my emotions. For the first time, I felt like a secure, sheltered daughter of the most wonderful Dad I could ever hope to have.

The Father longs to give this same reassuring, fatherly protection to each of His children who need His help to feel this safe.

He's a Dad we can Trust

If we had an earthly father who didn't keep his word, this betrayal taught us that we can't trust anyone. An incident when I was eleven years old is how this loss happened for me.

"Do you want to go to the movies?" Pop asked my sister and me on a rainy Saturday afternoon.

"Yes!" we said excitedly. "But will you stay with us, Pop?" I asked him. I still remembered the day he broke his promise and left us in the park until late at night.

"Yes, we'll have a great time together," he assured me.

I smiled happily at the thought of spending time with Pop and trusted him to keep his word to me this time.

Moments later we boarded a bus to take us to the movies. The ride took much longer than I expected as we traveled to a theatre a long way from where we lived. I didn't mind being so far from home because my father was with me. That made me feel safe.

When we arrived, we found seats very close to the front. Pop sat down next to me. I smiled contentedly as I snuggled close to him. The lights went out and the movie, "The House of Wax," flashed on the screen. Not long after it began, I realized it was a very scary movie. I never watched that type of movie because I was so easily frightened and I already had horrifying nightmares just about every night.

I pulled away from Pop.

The dark sounds of the music filled me with dread. I gasped as a man's face cracked into pieces. Underneath was a grotesque corpse. I screamed and turned to bury my face in Pop's shoulder. He was gone.

I desperately wanted to run out of the theatre and look for him. Yet I was too afraid to move.
So I covered my eyes and forced myself to stay in my seat.

"I wonder where Pop went?" I said to myself. "He promised he'd stay with us this time. He promised..."

The movie finally ended and I rushed up the aisle to search for my father. He was nowhere to be found. We and I waited and waited. Once again we were hungry just wanted to go home. But this was not possible. We were too far away to even know how to get there.

So I pressed my forehead against a cold window and stared at the cars as they whizzed by outside.

"Where are you, Pop?" I wondered. "Please come back..."

Hours later he returned.

"I couldn't stay," Pop said rather guiltily. "I had something I had to go take care of..."

"But you promised," I said with a hurt voice.

He merely motioned for me to be still and follow him as he walked briskly toward the bus stop. We sat a long time on the bench without saying a word. I wrapped my arms tightly around myself in a frantic effort to keep warm. But no matter how hard I tried to help myself, I couldn't stop shivering in the cold winter wind. Finally a dimly lit bus pulled up in front of us and I sat by a window next to Pop in strained silence while I turned my face away from him.

This time I was too hurt to even cry.

There were other moments when my father didn't keep his word to me.

The disillusionment from these shattering betrayals of my trust seriously affected me as I grew older. I ended up choosing to be close to men who treated me the same way Pop did. I should never have trusted them.

But I did.

Only when I began to understand that God is a Father whom I can trust did the cruel wounds from Pop begin to go away. Then as time went on and I let Him love me like a Dad, I experienced that He never makes a promise He will not keep. He never builds up our hopes only to let us down. I also grew stronger in the "new me" the more I hung on to the reassuring love in these words:

"My child,

Whenever you run to Me for refuge, you can take new courage because you can hold on to what I promise you with confidence. This solid confidence that I give you as your Father is a strong and trustworthy anchor for your soul so that you can always feel secure in My love for you.

So take new courage. You can hold on tight to the hope you have in Me. I will not let you down. I promise you I won't ever betray you trusting Me.

- Your Father who can be depended on to keep My promise to never abandon you"

Isaiah 28:16, 54:10 NLT/NIV/NASB
Joshua 23:14 NASB, Hebrews 6:18-19, 10:23 NLT

Jeremiah 31:3, Titus 1:2, Psalm 89:33-34, 9:10, 94:14 NLT
Hebrews 13:5, Deuteronomy 4:31 NLT

As this very new way of thinking became more and more a part of me, the seemingly insurmountable mountain of mistrust that was buried in my heart began to change.

Eventually I had the courage to try trusting those few people whom I felt were alright to let that far into my heart.

This meant I was taking the risk of getting hurt. There was no way to completely avoid that. It's just not possible.

But what hugely helped was that I had grown in so many ways, the people I was drawn to for personal relationship had drastically changed. They were actually kindred with the far healthier person I had become.

Experiencing this happening was so encouraging.

It was monumentally exciting!

Only God's kind, consistent, safe love for me as my Dad could make such an amazing transformation possible.

Chapter Four

WE NEED A MOM

I grew up in a home where there were no tender moments of closeness to my mother. I only remember harshness and cold rejection. Yet a new world opened up to me that I never dreamed was possible when the Word revealed to me God loves us not only as a Dad, but also as a caring mother.

If God had not become the Comforter to my troubled soul, the part of me that only a mother's love can touch never would have been restored.

What this revelation from the Bible did for me was a miracle!

It healed places in my soul that had been ravaged by my mother's rejection that felt irreversibly ruined. So with an incredibly grateful heart, I've often said to the Father:

"Your words have been my only source of hope. Truly I rejoice in Your Word like one who has found a great treasure. Because of Your mercy and compassion, you *do* send Your Word into our lives to heal us and deliver us from our destruction."

Psalm 119:114, 162 NLT
Psalm 107:20 NASB

If you are hurting because your mother couldn't love you, how I hope for you that the insights in this chapter will help the broken places in your heart. To sincerely encourage you, no words can adequately express how much what you are about to read is capable of transforming a deeply troubled soul that has not known a mother's love into one filled with joy and an amazing, miraculous peace.

God longs to Comfort us

As a child, the cry of my heart was, "Won't someone please love me?" But the older I grew, the more painfully aware I became of the crushing realization that when I was born, no one wanted me. Not even my mother. Because I felt this way, the older I grew the more I was driven to find someone to fulfill my need to be wanted by someone. But no one can satisfy a longing for what we missed out on as a child. Consequently, whenever this is what I tried to find, the more I ended up in one abusive relationship after another.

Nothing anyone did for me could ever change the fact that my mother didn't want me.

Then one day I made the discovery that God wanted me. He loves each of His children while we are in our mother's womb.

He even feels that way about us all the days of our life, just like a loving earthly mother feels toward her child.

That awakening began when I realized the significance of this promise by Jesus:

"I will ask the Father, and He will give you another Comforter so that He may remain with you forever."
John 14:16 AMP

Then this tender message from the Holy Spirit deepened my understanding of this Comforter that Jesus asked His Father to send to us.

"Dear child of Mine,

I made all the delicate, inner parts of your body and knit you together in your mother's womb. I was there, with you before you were born.

Even when your mother was pregnant with you, I already had wonderful plans for you and a purpose that would fulfill the deepest longings of your soul.

Then I watched you with such a tender love as you grew up and became a beautiful jewel even though so much in life was hurting you.

Please know that I have seen how you have suffered and My heart has ached for you. I don't want you to have to live another moment feeling like you missed out on a mother's love.

I want to comfort you as a loving mother does. I truly do, My child.

So please give Me a chance to do that for you because you have always been a wanted, deeply loved child by Me.

- The Holy Spirit who longs to give you all the comfort from a mother that you missed out on"

Isaiah 66:12-13, 46:3, 41:9 AMP/NASB/NLT
Isaiah 42:14-16, 46:3-4, 49:15-16, 40:11 NLT/NASB
Psalm 71:6, 139:13, 15-16, 27:10 NLT,
Ezekiel 16:4-7 NLT

Well, I did give the Holy Spirit that chance He asked for. This proved to be one of the best decisions I have ever made.

These are some of the insights He showed me that were life-changing.

The Holy Spirit really knows us

A loving mother has an intimate relationship with her child.

She is aware of him even when he is at a distance.

She understands how her child is feeling, including many of the thoughts he doesn't speak.

God loves us in this same amazing way.

He knows the number of hairs on our head. He understands our every thought and feeling.

He's continually aware of where we are and He even knows what we are going to say before we speak.

These are His reassuring words that let us know that this **is** how the Holy Spirit does care about us:

> "I have examined your heart. I know everything about you. I know when you sit down and when you stand up. I know your every thought when you are far away. Every moment, I know where you are."
>
> Psalm 139:1-3 NLT

God sings over us

When my children were little, I tucked them into bed at night and sang to them until they fell asleep.

One day through this verse in Zephaniah the Holy Spirit showed me that He also sings over us. And through His songs He calms us with His love, just like a mother's song calms her young child:

> "I will rejoice over you with great gladness. I will take great delight in you. With My love, I will calm all your fears. I will quiet you with My love. I will exult over you by singing a happy song. I will rejoice over you with singing."
>
> Zephaniah 3:17 NLT/KJV

He saves our Tears

I cried myself to sleep many a night growing up.

They were always private, lonely tears. My mother never hugged me or held me in her arms when I needed to be comforted. She never wiped away my tears.

This loss colored every day of my life with a sadness that never went away.

But now I never have to cry alone again.

This is how the Holy Spirit helped me to understand Him in this really new way:

"I will wipe away all your tears.

I keep track of all your sorrows. I've collected all your tears in My bottle. I've recorded each one in My book."

Isaiah 25:8, Psalm 56:8 NLT

God Understands

When I was a child I often sat alone on our old wooden porch, wrapped my arms around my knees and hugged them tightly to my chest as I thought to myself, "I wish Mom would come and spend time with me today. Maybe, just this once she will come, even if only for a minute."

But she never came. The special times of feeling close to my mother never happened for us.

"I'm too busy," she inevitably screamed at me with a shrill, harsh voice. As a result, a frightening, confusing emptiness gripped me. A tormenting loneliness hovered over me my entire childhood like a dark, oppressive shadow. I grew into adulthood with a sadness that would never go away.

Yet that heartache is now completely gone. Now I walk around feeling loved by the most comforting Mother that anyone could ever hope to have.

What set my heart free was realizing that God always has time for us. He's filled with joy whenever we come into His presence and want to just be with Him. And we never have to beg Him to come and be close to us because He longs to be in our presence, too. When we call out to Him, He never ignores us. He never pushes us away. He is quick to listen. He is quick to draw us close to Him.

The Word tells us that this is **exactly** how God feels about us.

Through these compassionate words He longs for us to understand that this is how He loves us:

"My child,

I care about what happens to you. I have compassion on you and with a love that never changes and never ends.

I'm always concerned for you and when you need My help, I will always come to help you.

Every moment of every day, I'm here for you as a shelter from any storm and any wind of difficulty and distress. So I will surely listen to your cries and comfort you. I will not reject you. I will not abandon you.

I will only respond, instantly, to the sound of your cries, just as surely as the arrival of dawn or the coming of rains in early spring.

I will never ignore your suffering.

I won't turn and walk away because I love you so much that I have chosen you for Myself as My own special treasure.

- Your understanding Comforter who is here for you every moment of your life and cares about you more than you could ever imagine"

Ezekiel 36:9 NLT, Isaiah 32:2, 43:4 NASB
Psalm 94:14, 135:4. 10:17, 22:24, 35:27 NLT
1 Peter 5:7, Hosea 6:3 NLT, Isaiah 30:19, 54:8 NLT

God gives us a Home to come back to when life Hurts

A loving mother can't rest until she knows that her children are doing well. To her dying breath, her desire is that each child finds a happy, full life. If one of them needs help and it's in her child's best interest for her to provide it, she will sacrifice, even greatly, in order to be there for him.

Sometimes what an adult needs from his mother is a supportive place to temporarily stay while he re-establishes his life.

At other times of crisis or bruising pain, that home is not necessarily a physical one. It's a place a person can come back to in his heart where he knows, no matter what, his mother loves him. She cares about what happens to him and she wants the best for him. In the consolation of that unchanging certainty, her love becomes a home away from home. It's a comforting, safe haven for his battered soul.

The following story illuminates how completely this place of emotional refuge was missing in the relationship with my mother.

Once my father died, life improved dramatically for Mom. She remarried and had a new life with ample finances. She had a lovely home, new friends and she even took pride in her appearance. Even though life got easier for her, she still had no feelings toward her children that are a natural part of being a mother.

The older I grew, the more I was convinced that if I was drowning and she had the only lifeline to throw to me so that I was safe, she wouldn't throw it. She would walk away from me and let me drown.

For example, I turned to my mother for a physical place of refuge when I left the convent, only to have her cruelly push me away. Although I was homeless and struggling to make an overwhelmingly difficult adjustment to life outside the convent, I was not welcome in her home.

She did give me some pretty clothes to wear. This hugely encouraged me. I had never worn anything that lovely. But a month later she insisted that I give them all back to her although I was destitute.

I desperately needed a mother's support at that critical crossroad in my life. Her cold rejection plunged me into a frightening, turbulent sea of disastrous choices and frantic despair.

Seven years went by.

I found myself catapulted into another crossroads in my life. Once again, Mom could not be that safe place for my heart.

A painful, disheartening conversation with her was especially shattering. I had just ended a violently abusive marriage. In the midst of feeling scared about starting a new life on my own, I was also trying to grapple with the trauma from my husband's recent attempt to kill me.

This is what unfolded that crushed me...

"Mom, he violently choked me," I told her on the phone as my voice trembled uncontrollably. "I was so frightened. But I've left him. I finally know that's what I need to do."

She listened in cold silence to my distress.

"I have no one to turn to," I continued. "I have no friends. I was always so ashamed of the abuse that I didn't let anyone get close to me. I..."

"You'll have to work it out for yourself," she abruptly said before I could finish my sentence. "I can't help you."

After an awkward silence, I ended the conversation. This was the last time I asked my mother for help. I had to face that I had absolutely no one who loved me.

Yet no matter how old we are, we still need to know we have a mom who cares about us. When a mother's love has always been missing, the pain of that loss does not get less as the years go by. It actually hurts more the older we get.

If the Holy Spirit hadn't healed my broken heart, the rejection from my mother could have destroyed my mind and poisoned my soul for the rest of my life.

But that didn't happen.

Instead this is what God mercifully showed me that set me free. It's a message of love for anyone who needs this kind reassurance:

"My child,

I make a home for you whenever you are lonely because I am merciful. I will support you.

I will be a sanctuary for you.

Whenever you need a home in the comforting shelter of My presence, I will be that welcoming, understanding refuge for you.

I promise that no matter what is happening in your life, I will look after you and take good care of you. I will even make a pathway in your wilderness so that you always will know the way for you to be able to come home to Me in your heart and find the peace you need.

I will do all this for you so that you can hide beneath the shadow of My wings until any violent storm in your life is past. Tears of joy will stream down your face as I show you the way back home to Me in My presence. You will be radiant because of the many gifts I give you. Your life will feel like a watered garden.

- Your Comforter and your Home that you can always come back to whenever you need Me to be here for you"

Psalm 68:6 NASB/MOFFATT
Isaiah 42:6, 8:14, 43:19 NLT/NASB

Jeremiah 3:12, Hosea 14:8, Joel 3:16 NLT
Psalm 57:1, 91:4, 9-19, Isaiah 25:4 NLT
Jeremiah 31:9, 31:12, 46:27

As a result of this comforting mother's love from the Holy Spirit, I finally saw that I *do* have a home to come back to in God's heart whenever life hurts.

No matter what happens, I have this place of refuge and comforting peace.

The more this realization sunk in, the more a crippling sense of loss from my relationship with my earthly mother left me. The damage from her abandonment no longer could poison my soul. It stopped influencing my choices in relationships.

Her rejection had no power over me anymore. Instead I began to live every moment in the sheltering presence of my God and He has been that safe harbor for me, over and over, since I was thirty-one.

What's amazing is each time I have ever needed a refuge in the haven of such a kind, caring love, He's never been too busy to help me. He's never pushed me away. I only receive a warm welcome and the full, unwavering support of a mother's comfort. Consequently, everything that I lost as a result of Mom's rejection has been given back to me.

God restored my health, both physically and emotionally.

He took my wounded, broken heart and gave me a new one.

It's as if all the tragic loss from my mother never occurred because none of the pain and loss even matters anymore.

When I think about her, I'm not sad.

All the years of experiencing a mother's comfort from the reassuring understanding of God's love has set me free.

Chapter Five

I HAD TO FORGIVE

Excerpt from Ruth's book:
"Revival on the Horizon"

By the time I was thirty years old, I experienced every type of brutally scarring abuse.

As a result, I hated men. I feared and mistrusted women. I never felt completely safe with anyone.

Frightening nightmares terrified me whenever I tried to sleep. An irrational panic consumed my thoughts. Fear imprisoned me. Haunting memories bombarded me. Remembering the painful, graphic details of the terrible things that had happened to me and my brother and sister constantly replayed in my mind. Rage simmered inside me. At times it came out in uncontrollable explosions of destructive anger. Thoughts of killing myself consumed me.

No one knew about the terrifying abuse I was living with or how I felt about anything. Emotional honesty didn't feel safe at all. All of this caused me to shrink back from reality. I isolated myself. There was the smiling person people saw in public, and the disturbed one who lived inside of me. The stress of all this began to affect me physically. A doctor told me I had the beginnings of many serious health issues and I had better do something about what was going on in my life that could cause all this damage. But as I listened to him warn me, I saw no way I could get free from the torment I was hiding from everyone.

After being betrayed and violated, over and over, as a child by those who were supposed to be safe for me to trust, fragile places on the inside of me had died a long time ago.

The damage felt irreversible.

In the midst of this personal nightmare, I never thought it would be possible to put it all behind me and not have it control my life anymore. Yet that transformation did happen.

What took place is a message of hope for all who ache to be set free from devastating pain and fully enter into the fullness of the Father's destiny for them.

I Forgive

No child wants to hate his parents. When we do, something dies in our soul that we seriously need to be a whole person. That death remains until we forgive. If we refuse to, this choice is deadly. It can cause us physical illness and even thrust us into the alarming, dark shadows of being emotionally disturbed.

This is how that happened for me.

A long time before I became a Christian, I made up my mind I'd never forgive my parents for the horrible things they did to me.

Consequently, when I was saved at twenty-nine, the agony of my pain didn't stop. It actually got worse because I refused to stop being bitter. The poison of this destructive choice affected every part of my life. Through my toxic example, my daughter learned that the way you react to people who hurt you is to hate them. Eventually that hatred included me. My disastrous decision to not forgive catapulted me to the brink of a serious mental collapse.

After I had been a Christian for about two years, my world came crashing down all around me. I heard voices, but no one was actually speaking to me. Late at night I was afraid to walk past the living room. I was sure that a man was lurking in the shadows waiting to attack me. But whenever I rushed to turn on the lights, no one was there. I often woke up in a cold sweat from terrifying nightmares. In these haunting dreams, my ex-husband kept coming back to kill me.

During the day, a chilling apprehension obsessed me. Every time my children walked outside to play, I shuddered with out of control fear that they would be killed.

After one of these attacks of anxiety, I retreated to my bedroom. As I lay rigidly on my bed, I was convinced that someone was coming stealthily down the hallway toward my room. My heart raced and my body stiffened under the cold sheets. I was too terrified to make a sound. I strained to listen for footsteps. But there was only silence, except for my muffled breathing. I pulled the blanket tight under my chin and stared at the partially opened door.

"He's going to kill me!" I screamed within me as I frantically gripped the blanket. "I know there's someone out there and he's going to kill me."

I couldn't move. I could barely breathe. My disturbed mind was convinced that an intruder was there.

The alarming history of insanity on both sides of my family now raced through my mind.

"I'm going crazy," I thought, "just like so many people in my family. I'm going to end up like one of them. I'm losing my mind!"

My life was spinning out of control.

The evil forces that were trying to destroy me kept battering me with terrifying thoughts. I felt like I was suffocating in a dark tunnel of frightening panic. I tried to stop the downward spiral. But I couldn't push back the darkness that was now overtaking me. I was painfully aware that at any moment I could cross over into a place of so much mental confusion that I wouldn't be able to come back to reality.

"Oh God," I cried out. "Help me! Please help me!"

The Father's response was immediate. But it **wasn't** comforting like I had expected.

"Ruth," He told me, "you must forgive everyone who has ever hurt you, especially your mother. The hatred toward your mother is the bitter root that is destroying you."

I resisted.

"After everything my mother has done to me," I vehemently said, "I have every right to hate her. I'll forgive everyone else, but I will never forgive my mother!"

But God warned me:

"If you don't forgive her, your hatred will destroy you. And I won't be able to help you."

I jumped up from my bed, stood in the middle of the room, and shook with loud sobs. My mind was already dangerously close to slipping away from me. I couldn't go on living the way I was feeling for another second. I was determined to hang on to life as I lifted my arms like a young, trusting child.

"Oh God," I cried out. "I don't feel any forgiveness toward Mom. But I will do what You are telling me to do. I choose to forgive her. In the name of Jesus I forgive her." At first I said these words completely by faith.

I felt nothing at all.

But as I made the decision to speak them over and over, my feelings toward my mother changed. Suddenly vivid scenes from my childhood flashed through my mind. I recalled her bending over the kitchen sink, moaning in pain; being stiff and white as a corpse on her bed in her darkened room, her countenance clouded with despair; lying collapsed on the kitchen floor, unable to speak; screaming at me every time I tried to talk to her, "Shut up! Leave me alone," pushing me away whenever I tried to be close to her.

I covered my face with trembling hands and wept as I faced with full honesty how much all this had hurt me.

THE TRIP TO FREEDOM

I then told God all about it, holding nothing back as a lifetime of pain exploded out of my soul. Suddenly, something amazing happened. My heart began to ache for my mother. Instead of seeing her as the person who had caused me so much suffering, I was able to look at her through the eyes of the Father. Compassion for her hopelessness pierced my heart. She knew I was suffering all those years when I was growing up. But she was in too much pain herself to have anything left to give to anyone. It took all she had to just survive.

Moments later, a healing I never thought was possible began to touch the most broken places in my soul. "I not only forgive her, Lord," I then told Him, "but for the first time I can finally say I love her. I forgive everyone who has ever hurt me, even though I have no feelings about doing that. I'm just deciding because I don't want to hang on to any of it anymore."

I learned I could do all this by **choice** when I read these surprising words:

> "**You** must change your heart and life. I am kind to you so that you can do this. So **choose** this day a blessing or a curse. I urge you to choose life in order that you may live."
>
> Acts 3:19 NCV, Romans 2:4 NCV
> Deuteronomy 30:19 NASB

I'll never forget how it struck me that God didn't say, "**Feel** this day a blessing or a curse." He said choose."

He also didn't say that **He** was in charge of doing all the changing in me. He put a lot of that responsibility on me.

Then as I decide to obey His Word in my choices, He can come in with a flood of help, just as He promises in these incredibly reassuring words: "There is no one like the God of Israel. He rides across the heavens to help you, across the skies in majestic splendor." Deuteronomy 33:26 NLT

What's sad is many people think that if they don't feel it, then it's not real forgiveness. As a result, they are trapped in their bitterness, with no way to end it. So I'll always be grateful that the Word makes it clear we only have to **decide** to forgive.

This decision can set us free from hatred, even if we feel nothing at all.

But for me all of this was the easy part. After I forgave my mother and everyone who had ever hurt me, I was only able to move on with my life when every day, many times a day, I made the determined decision to not let my mind go back to thinking about the past. I learned I had to do this from Paul when he declared:

> "Brethren, I do not regard myself as having laid hold of it yet; but one thing I do. **Forgetting** what lies behind, and reaching forward to what lies ahead, I press on toward the goal for the prize of the upward call of God in Christ Jesus."
>
> Philippians 3:13-14 NLT/NASB

Paul even explained what we have to do so that we are able to "forget," since even after we forgive those destructive thoughts can still come at our mind and trouble us all over again if we allow it.

Through these practical instructions I began to understand that Word-based "forgetting" means refusing to **think** about the hurts anymore:

> "Fix your thoughts on what is true and honorable and right. Think about things that are pure and lovely and a **good** report. Think about things that are excellent and worthy of praise. Practice these things and the God of peace will be with you. And cast down imaginations and every high thing that exalts itself against the knowledge of God. Bring into captivity **every thought** to the obedience of Christ."
>
> 2 Corinthians 10:5 KJV
> Philippians 4:8-9 NLT/NASB

As a result of learning all this from Paul, every time the oppressive remembering of past hurts tried to bombard my mind, I did all I could, just as fast as possible, to stop those thoughts "in their tracks." At the same time, I changed what I was thinking about to a "good report" such as:

What I was grateful for

A scripture that helped me to have peace

Simple, from the heart, childlike words to
God about how much I love Him.

The Father helped me see that I also had to **stop talking** about the hurts because "the words I speak can cause death to come on my life and emotions." Proverbs 18:21 NCV

If that happens, the horrible pain can torment us all over again. Then we have to battle the haunting memories and what a waste of emotional energy that is. I know because there were times at the beginning of this new way of living when I did allow myself to talk about the old "stuff." But I learned very quickly that this was a big mistake and it was awful to have to fight against all the old stuff until I got back to a place of peace again.

At first, hanging on to my breakthrough was exhausting. I had to stop my thoughts and change them to a "good report" an unbelievable number of times all day long because my mind had such a life-long habit of endlessly rehearsing the hurts.

To help me, I wrote down a few verses and kept them with me wherever I went. Then whenever I was taken off guard by one of these really difficult moments in my mind, I was immediately able to read them. I also memorized a few that helped me the most whenever I thought about them.

At night when I had troubling dreams, I could wake up and easily change what I was focusing on to those comforting verses.

Yet, I also discovered that no matter how diligent I was in dealing with the damage from my past, I still could get hit unexpectedly with disturbing reminders. At first whenever that happened, it felt like everything was just as bad as it used to be. Sometimes this caused me to question if I had truly forgiven or even if I had actually been healed. However, as fast as possible I told myself that all of this was a horrible lie and a vicious, demonic attack to rob me of my peace. I also very firmly reminded myself that if I allowed these lies to stay in my thoughts, I would be dragged back into a place of torment and darkness and I would be doing that to myself.

So just as quickly as if someone had thrown a hot potato at me to catch, I learned to stop negative thoughts by refusing to let my mind think them.

What's really encouraging is that as time passed, these struggles became less intense.

They occurred less often.

Gradually, being whole and healthy became my new "normal."

The poisonous venom of my hatred was gone. In all the caverns of my soul where resentment once reigned, a light now shined.

This took care of the past.

Yet then I had to learn how to deal with new, significantly painful moments that occur in the present.

For example, Mom never changed the way she treated me. Her rejection actually became more cruel. I would drive five hundred miles to visit her. After I had been with her only a few minutes she would coldly say, "You can leave now. Goodbye." Each time her pushing me away brought back an avalanche of all the pain from a lifetime of her doing this to me.

But I remembered to react to the hurt as if it was a "hot potato," by forgiving so fast that bitterness didn't have the power to get back into my heart and rob me of my peace.

Likewise, during those new times of devastating sadness and a raw sense of loss in my relationship with my mother, I also firmly reminded myself:

"No matter how much I want Mom to love me, I can't make that happen. I will only be destroyed if I open the door again and allow myself to need her love. So I choose again to run to the kind love of God." Each time I made this decision, the Lord always reminded me: "I will comfort you just like a caring mother does for her child." Isaiah 66:13 NASB

At the same time, I had to put the new mountain of horrible grief behind me. I was able to do that by once again being completely real with myself and with God about how devastated I felt. Then just as soon as I could, that **same day** if at all possible, I passionately obeyed the Father who told me:

"**Forget** all that.

It is **nothing** compared to what I am going to do."

Isaiah 43:18-19 NLT, Philippians 3:12-14 NASB

These choices made it possible for me to swiftly shut the door on any new rejection from Mom and not allow it to have any power over my life. These determined decisions also kept me from feeling all over again that I had a gaping hole in my heart where a mother's love needed to be. Instead, I continued to walk in the comforting kindness of the Holy Spirit every time I got to the other side of one of these really hard experiences.

But my mother was so determined to push me out of her life that even as she faced her death, she had no room in her heart for me. She ended her days just as she had lived them, not wanting to know me or even say goodbye to me by telling my sister to never let me know she had died. To fulfill that promise, she completely disappeared from my life. I had no idea how to find her or mom. I didn't even know that my mother was gone until eight years after her death.

No words can sufficiently capture how much this hurt. Yet as I have been describing, I had learned what to do when new hurts happened and clearly understanding this is what protected my heart. So once again, I knew how to get to the other side of the overwhelming grief so that I could be at peace again. Consequently, the damage from her abandonment in no way was able to poison my soul. I was able to put the crippling sense of loss from this final, brutally cruel rejection behind me and once again embrace where the Father wanted me to go in my life. As a result, the lifetime of heartache from knowing my mother does not influence my choices in relationships. Her rejection has no power over me at all. It's as if all the tragic loss from my relationship with her never occurred. None of the pain she caused even matters to me anymore. I am loved by the best Dad in the whole world and I've found a home and a safe refuge for my heart in the kind and tender heart of God.

Yet the time to let go of all bitterness is before we make big mistakes in relationships and before we damage those we love with its toxic poison. That's why I wish I had found the liberating truth about forgiving when I was much younger. This would have changed the course of my life.

Chapter Six

LIBERATING HONESTY

Excerpt from Ruth's book:
"Revival on the Horizon"

Along this Journey of growing in a very personal relationship with the Father, I've realized that overcoming the pain caused by a hurtful past is **not** found in "stuffing" it, ignoring it, or minimizing what affected us.

What helps us become whole and then move on into everything God has planned for us is being fully honest with **ourselves** about how we are hurting, and be **just as real** with the Father about it also.

I found this freeing insight in the life of David.

He was cruelly rejected by his father, as if he didn't exist. He was publicly degraded by his brother, Eliab who spoke demeaning words to him in front of others. His friend, Saul betrayed him and viciously turned on him. He had many men killed in battle so that David could take the wife of one of them. He also made serious mistakes with his children that caused him more and more heartache the older they got. So there was in many ways overwhelming pain in David that he had to face and overcome. But what I find remarkable is how he didn't hide any of his feelings from himself or from God. Rather He faced them honestly.

He even said these pretty surprising things to God:

"Lord, why do You stand so far away? Why do You hide when I need You the most? How long will You forget me? How long will You look the other way? How long must I struggle with anguish in my soul and sorrow in my heart every day?

My God, my God, why have You forsaken me? Why do You remain so distant? Why do You ignore my cries for help? Why have You tossed me aside?"

Psalm 10:1, 13:1-2, 22:1-2, 43:2 NLT

It's also amazing to me that God never scolded David for saying any of that to Him.

He was never upset about the blunt honesty.

He knew it would help David feel closer to Him. So in response, the Father was only there for His son. He only treated this broken, hurting man with compassionate understanding.

Then **after** his serious failures, God still called David a "man after His own heart" and he fulfilled his destiny as King.

Yet for some people, what's affecting them is so unclear that they can't be honest with themselves and with God like David was. They need help seeing what is troubling them before they can do this and Word-based counseling can be the Father's merciful provision so that He can help them to be set free.

However what saddens me is I've known countless men and women who have received this help. But they **don't stop** analyzing their pain. Instead they continue talking and thinking about the hurts.

Those I've known who decided to go this direction as a way to cope with their past are just about all still stuck there. The years have gone by and they've never been able to put it all behind them and begin to live.

They also have become increasingly more self-focused because so much of their time is centered on thinking about themselves and their efforts to get healed from their hurts. It may even seem to them that this doing all this is wise, even helpful.

But it's a quest that seriously hinders their ability to have the rewarding relationships the Father wants for them to experience in the present. Because these mutually healthy relationships are not possible when someone gets caught up in putting way too much energy, time and effort into thinking about themselves in an endless attempt to "fix" their lives.

This self-focus also shuts down intimacy with God.

When they try to worship, often all they can see is themselves, their pain and what they need from Him. And He does very much care about our needs. But, when any believer turns his time of being with God into mainly thinking about himself and what He can do for him, this is a one-way, self-centered relationship.

Yet **no** relationship can be close if it's about one person thinking mainly about themselves, their needs and their struggles.

This will destroy closeness with **anyone**, including God.

Sometimes people keep looking at their past because they want to recall what they can't remember.

They think that's going to help their heart to heal.

But in all my decades of ministry, including extensive pastoral counseling trying to help people understand what is troubling them that happened a long time ago, I've never known anyone who benefitted from trying to get their mind to remember what it does not recall. Instead I've only seen this effort devour precious years of their life. Sadly, what a person is searching for, even if they don't realize it, is a way to regain what they've lost. But none of these efforts can ever give back to them the love they missed out on. Worse yet, trying to remember what the mind does not recall will cause what they do remember to become even more painfully raw.

Meanwhile, God's plan for them is shipwrecked. Living life to the fullest is on hold until all the endless levels of hurts are examined and the pain of the past is able to rob them all over again.

Then, even if they start to do better, as soon as another hurt comes along or another troubling reminder of the past affects them, they often think they are not "healed." So they have to return to the analyzing and talk about these new hurts.

To be honest, I have many years of my childhood that I can't remember at all and I'm hugely grateful for those missing pieces in my memories.

I consider what I can't recall from my past a gift of mercy and kindness from God.

I celebrate that He did this for me.

I also decided not to even try to remember any of it.

I just wanted to face the pain of the past that I did very clearly remember and then put it all behind me so that I could move on with where God wanted to take me.

This decision made it possible for me to pour my whole heart into what was ahead of me that a loving Father wanted me to enjoy living to the fullest for Him. However, if I had gone the direction of trying to figure out every detail of my past, including trying to remember what I had no memory of, I'd still be working on it. None of this moving forward would have been possible.

So I'm overwhelmingly grateful that the Bible **doesn't** tell us to keep on trying to uncover every detail of our past hurts or keep on thinking and talking about them.

This is what a loving, kind Father tells us to focus on:

> "Let us run with endurance the race that God has set before us. We do this by keeping our eyes on Jesus on whom our faith depends from start to finish."
>
> Hebrews 12:1-2 NLT

But we **can't** keep our eyes on Jesus when we continue to focus on what is negative, such as our past. It's just not possible. Devastating experiences are that powerful in how they can keep our thoughts riveted on the losses in our life.

Yet when we honestly face our hurts, and we forgive, and decide "enough is enough" by refusing to think and talk about them, then we can enter into a whole new realm of freedom.

In that new place where the past no longer has the power to rob us, what happened to us that caused us so much heartache can't control our lives anymore. We also get to experience our loving Dad giving us a new beginning in His "future and hope" for us, just as He encourages us will happen in these deeply reassuring words:

The Father says, "Please come."

"Oh My beloved child, please come and be with Me whenever you are having a hard time. I promise you as your very real Dad that each time you do, not only will you be in My presence where you will be helped in very encouraging ways, but how I long to be in **your** presence.

Whenever you come, for even just a moment at a time, I will comfort you as no one else can.

But as you do, I need for you to lay down all the thoughts about yourself and your pain and difficulties, and come to just be with Me. Then as your Father who loves you more than you could ever hope for or imagine, I will come to be with you. And in the places you are still hurting, I can heal you, and it won't take years and years. Instead, with each touch of My kind presence upon you, you can go from healing to healing.

Each time you come to be close to Me, I also promise I will refresh your weary, broken places so that when you turn and face your life again, you will be amazed. The circumstances may still be exactly the same.

But everything will look different because you have experienced how understanding I am about how you are feeling.

So I say to you, please come often into My presence.

As you do, I will revive My destiny for you that you've been feeling so discouraged about, wondering if it will ever happen. In that closeness with Me, you will be strengthened because I can show you what I'm doing in your life, your calling, your destiny, your work, your ministry. As you enter into that most sacred place to just be with Me, I will anoint you afresh with my prophetic anointing. I will open up to you the secrets on My heart and reveal to you what I'm doing among My people, and for the hurting and lost of the nations.

As you bow your heart, your knees, your whole life before Me with humble, repentant brokenness and as you die to every mindset that is holding you back and defeating you, I am going to do a new thing in your life. My child, it's already begun.

So My child, when you awaken each morning, before you do anything else, please want to be with Me. Throughout each day, talk to Me as a dearest friend does with his dearest friend.

When you put your head on the pillow each night, fall asleep telling Me you love Me. But not in fancy words. Just in childlike, simple, from the heart, sincere words.

And if you wake up in the night troubled, anxious, or afraid, instantly start talking to Me. Begin to think about My presence and wanting to be close to Me.

I will come to be with you. I will come in a heartbeat. You will feel safe and protected by My love for you. You will be able to peacefully fall asleep in My sheltering presence.

To reassure you, I fully understand as your Dad that there will be bumps along the way. There will be mistakes.

That's why this Journey of you fulfilling My plan for your life is **not** about you being perfect. I already know as your Father that there will be times when you will need My help to be restored to the fullness of all this because of the mistakes you make along the way.

All I ask of you is that you sincerely try and seek Me with a humble heart.

Then, even when you have 'blown it' and you are struggling, you will still be one of My servants through whom I will show forth My glory, just like happened to David, and Peter, and Paul.

So please, stay close to Me, no matter what happens in your life and you will be one of My godly ones who will bless Me. You will speak of the glory of My Kingdom and talk of My power. To make known to the sons of men My mighty acts and the glory of the majesty of My Kingdom.

- Your Father and your Dad"

Psalm 145:10-12 NASB

Chapter Seven

REGRETS

Excerpt from Ruth's book:
"Revival on the Horizon"

The worst kind of pain to get over is often our regrets.

That's what happened to me.

Although I had forgiven everyone else in my life, I didn't know how to give that same grace and mercy to myself.

Mainly because I didn't know how to stop the agony of wishing I had done things differently when I was raising my children. I kept getting battered by remembering that after they were abused in my first marriage, I put them in another unsafe home with my second husband where they were hurt in even more horrifically damaging ways.

I began to find my way out of this torment when I was able to see how God looked at my failures as a mother. This is what He showed me. It is for anyone who needs this same reassuring and really different perspective:

"You couldn't have tried harder to be a good mom. It just was not possible. You had no more you could give.

So you need to stop judging yourself by what you now realize they needed from you. You need to see that it just couldn't happen back then.

You also need to encourage yourself that you **did** try your very best with what you were capable of giving to them at that time. This is how I see you. And it's how I, as your Dad, long for you to see yourself."

Once I let this kindness from the Father into my heart I finally was able to forgive myself. But I also experienced that though the guilt was gone, it didn't mean that thinking about my regrets wouldn't hurt anymore. For years the holidays still stirred up a world of heartache any time I was hit with what I had lost in my relationships with my children. But once I forgave myself then the pain was different. When I was full of guilt, the torment wouldn't go away. Yet now I was able to work through the emotions and get to the other side of them, and more and more quickly. I did that by reminding myself:

"I can't change the choices that I made in the past. I can only make healthy choices in the present."

Then I switched the heartbreaking thoughts to anything that gave me comfort and hope. I knew it was critical that I make this choice as soon as possible because I had spent so many years wishing I had done things differently that it was easy for me to be devastated by painful memories if I let them stay in my thoughts. So I had to be vigilantly careful not to allow myself to think about them.

Whenever they did flash through my mind uninvited and unexpectedly, I had to shut them down by **making** myself stop those thoughts and change them to whatever helped me to have the Father's comfort and peace.

During the years since this radical change in my life, I've often been strengthened by thinking about the life of Paul. He was a man who easily could have been mentally and emotionally destroyed by remembering his failures.

These are some of the horrific things he did:

Paul had the power to stop innocent Stephen from being stoned to death. But he stood there and let that man whose face shined like an angel be viciously killed.

Then after that death "a great wave of persecution began that same day. Saul went everywhere to devastate the church. He went from house to house, dragging out both men and women to throw them in jail."

After he was saved and serving the Father as an apostle, he wrote to the Corinthians how he felt about all this.

"I am the least worthy of the apostles and I am not fit or deserving to be called an apostle, because I once wronged and pursued and molested the church of God, oppressing it with cruelty and violence. You know what I was like when I followed the Jewish religion, how I violently persecuted the Christians.

I did my best to get rid of them.

I used to believe that I ought to do everything I could to oppose the followers of Jesus. Authorized by the leading priests, I caused many of the believers in Jerusalem to be sent to prison.

"I cast my vote against them when they were condemned to death. Many times I had them whipped in the synagogues to try to get them to curse Christ. I was so violently opposed to them that I even hounded them in distant cities of foreign lands."

1 Corinthians 15:9 AMP, Galatians 1:13
Acts 8:1-3, 26:9-11 NLT

This is a world of pain for any human being to overcome.

It's enough to haunt anyone with emotionally crippling guilt for the rest of their life.

But Paul got free!

He went on to fully live the Father's plan for him to make a difference in the lives of others. He did that by refusing to let his deeply regretted past destroy him by making up his mind to receive the Father's forgiveness. In response to that mercy, Paul found the courage to forgive himself. Then he made the hard choice to forget it all and move on with his life.

That is what I had to do also.

Chapter Eight

WHAT TO LOOK FOR WHEN DATING

When the emotions start happening in a dating relationship and the sexual attraction begins to cloud our judgment, it's way too easy to block out the warning signs that being involved with that person is a mistake.

Therefore, I learned the hard way that it is monumentally important to clearly understand **before** a relationship begins what qualities to look for in anyone you want to date.

This is a major way we can take seriously these sobering words of extremely important caution:

"Be shrewd as serpents and innocent as doves."
Matthew 10:16 NASB

To be shrewd means to have "down to earth," basic, objective common sense operating in our thinking so that it can guide us in our choices with people.

I also have found that anyone who has a history of choosing destructive relationships has a very difficult time having that shrewdness about who they get involved with. In the past, this was certainly true of me.

That's why God, as our Dad who wants the very best for us, does urge us in these compelling words:

> "Call out to Me and I will answer you. I will reveal to you what is hard and hidden, those things that you do not know. I will guide you along the best pathway for your life. I will advise you and watch over you. I will keep on guiding you with My counsel."
>
> Jeremiah 33:3 MOFFATT
> Psalm 32:8, 73:23 NLT

What's sad is when my dangerously abusive marriage ended, I begged God to help me see what I needed to know so that I could make very different choices about who I got involved with as a friend or as someone to date. The last thing in the world I wanted was to marry the wrong person again. Yet I foolishly rushed into another disastrous marriage. I was horrified when I discovered on our honeymoon that this man was far more cruel in his abuse than anything I had ever experienced in my entire life.

As time went on, and my children and I suffered horrifically, I felt God had betrayed me and angrily told Him:

> "I trusted You! Why did You allow this to happen to me? I told You I only wanted Your will. Why didn't You warn me? You are all powerful. Why didn't You stop me?"

Only years later did I grasp that God **did** warn me many times when I was dating this man that I needed to end my involvement with him. But I chose not to listen.

He even sent a trusted friend into my life who told me: "I guarantee if you marry him, you will regret it."

Yet I refused to slow down and at least consider if the Father was trying to protect me, and my children, from another serious mistake.

Consequently, we lived fourteen more years in a nightmare of the worst kinds of brutally scarring, heartbreaking, degrading abuse.

You may be saying, and understandably so,

> "How can anyone who is praying a lot about not wanting to end up in another abusive relationship still marry someone who had many alarming behaviors **before** she married him?"

The answer is simple.

I was already way too emotionally involved with this man to want to listen to anything that could affect my continuing the relationship.

So I blocked out all the Holy Spirit's efforts to get my attention.

How I hope that what happened to me can help others to remember how seriously important it is to make sure that you watch for behaviors that can help you know whether or not someone is a wise person to be friends with or to date.

I compiled this list to help you be aware of specifically what to look for:

Some of the qualities and behaviors which are warnings that a person could end up being a significant mistake to be friends with or to continue dating:

*In all cases "he" refers to **both** a woman or a man.*

You feel controlled, stifled, smothered.

You are not comfortable introducing this person to your friends.

You find yourself becoming more and more isolated from people who are close to you.

There are moments when you feel used, or worse yet, degraded if you are around him.

There are times when you don't feel free to be completely yourself when you are with him.

Often you don't fully relax when you are with him because you are concerned about how he will react to you.

More and more you hide from him your feelings.

You make excuses for his behaviors.

You allow him to tell you what to do.

You feel a responsibility to help him fix his problems.

He's often oblivious to your feelings and needs.

He has to have things his way or there is tension between you.

He tries to tell you what to do with your personal decisions.

He tries to control who you spend your time with.

He is often "down," depressed and negative about how he looks at life.

He likes it when you feel sorry for him.

He expects you to do things for him. But he bristles if you ask him to help you.

He does not like himself. He's insecure about who he is. You are constantly in the role of reassuring him, encouraging him, pumping up his low self-worth.

He doesn't really listen and take it to heart when you tell him that he has been unkind or hurtful to you. He explains away his negative behaviors. He expects you to accept his excuses for them.

He seems to feel he is always right. So it's always somehow your fault if you two have problems.

He's critical of you and says things that are unkind, though he may be quick to apologize. But he does not change. He does the same thing again, as if you never told him that it was a hurtful way to treat you.

He gets defensive when you are honest with him about something that is bothering you. So you find yourself feeling less and less comfortable being honest with him about how you are feeling if it involves something he said or did that was hurtful. You would rather be silent and "stuff" your feeling so you don't have to deal with his reactions if you try to be honest.

He dwells on past relationships and past hurts. He has not let go of the hurts of the past.

He is bitter.

He is a grudge holder.

He is quick to blame others for his past problems and does not take responsibility for them himself.

The positive qualities and behaviors that can help you when you are trying to decide if a relationship has the potential of being a good one for you to continue:

*In all cases "he" refers to **both** a woman or a man.*

You have fun with him. You laugh together.

He likes you just the way you are. He genuinely enjoys who you are.

He is just as supportive of your dreams and hopes and desires, as you are of his.

He's someone you feel you can trust. You relax around him. You can easily, comfortably, be yourself. You can talk to him as you would a good friend. You always feel you can be fully honest with him.

You sense that you have the same heart, same desires, and same longings about what matters the most to you.

He genuinely loves the Lord. You can pray with him. You share a spiritual closeness.

What's important to you matters to him, even if it's not something that personally matters to him all that much.

He cares very much about how you feel. Being kind to you and good to you matters a lot to this person.

You feel completely safe about being current with him about your feelings and about any hurts in the relationship.

If you tell him he's been hurtful, he's not defensive. He's sincerely sorry and you know that is what is happening if he makes a great deal of effort to not hurt you again in that same way.

If he's had an abusive background, he has come to a place of peace about it and has put it behind him. One way you can know this is if he doesn't need to talk about it. Not out of an effort to "stuff" it, but because he genuinely refuses to allow his past to rob his life in the present or negatively affect what the Father has for his future. As a result, he truly wants to focus on enjoying who you are and on the fun of your relationship with him and not on the hurts from his past.

Being aware of what I've just shared can hugely protect anyone who is single from making disastrous choices that can cause you terrible heartache.

Now let's continue on with our journey of seeing more practical insights that can help us understand how to stay on the path in our relationships that leads to freedom.

Chapter Nine

WHAT'S "NORMAL"

It isn't normal to be in constant emotional pain.

Yet if someone grows up in a family where abuse is happening, then at a young age he is learns an acceptance of it as just the way life is. This mixed up view of what to allow can affect all their personal relationships because when they grow up and begin to date, being mistreated feels "normal."

That is what happened to me. People being cruel was just the way life looked in our family. As a result, when I was dating my first husband, he hurt me physically, emotionally and verbally. He even degraded me sexually. Yet it never occurred to me to tell myself:

> "Something is really sick about this relationship. I need to end it immediately."

Instead, I accepted this man's indifference to my feelings.

I was frightened by his rage, but I didn't consider leaving him.

Despite his abusive treatment, I married him.

That's when I moved into familiar territory. Normal once again meant that every day I was going to hurt.

Even after I became a Christian and long after this frightening nightmare ended, I didn't see how unhealthy I was in my high tolerance for emotional pain. So I was actually shocked when I first saw that this is how strongly the Father feels about us being involved in a destructive personal relationship:

**"You are not to associate with anyone
who claims to be a Christian, yet is abusive.
Don't even eat with such people."**
1 Corinthians 5:11 NLT

The longer I walked hand in hand with my new Dad, the more I understood that this is exactly how He feels and that He's quite passionate about it. Then there came a day when this new way of looking at people changed my entrenched, warped ideas about what I should accept in any relationship.

That transformation became part of me when I decided, and really meant it, that the heavenly Father **doesn't** want us to accept being mistreated in our personal relationships anymore. He wants us to be honest about any mistreatment. He does not want us to simply allow it.

Yet life does hurt. There's no avoiding it completely. People hurt sometimes, no matter how healthy a relationship is.

But constant emotional turmoil in any personal relationship is **not** what God wants us to accept as alright. His desire for us is to help us have wisdom about **not allowing** that kind of way too often emotional pain. Even a loving earthly father feels this way toward his child and the Father is not going to care about us less than an earthly Dad.

Chapter Ten

TWO-WAY RELATIONSHIP

If I continue to accept in any personal relationship the role of a one-sided caring, I've become a parent to that person.

Yet I had spent most of my life taking on far too much responsibility for the other person's needs in a relationship, while at the same time accepting that my needs were not being considered hardly at all.

It was also quite illuminating to finally grasp that abusive people are thrilled to know someone who has this mixed up thinking because we are easily manipulated to feel sorry for them. As a result we easily feel bad if we ever hesitate to do what they need for us to do for them. We also are willing to care about their needs in sick, extreme, horribly unhealthy ways, while at the same time we are accepting of that person doing just about all the taking from us.

We even will tend to feel guilty about asking that they care about us also and are therefore quick to believe any criticism that we are selfish to want the relationship caring to go both directions.

Unfortunately, as a child this is how I learned to define love. I gave and gave to each of them. But I dared not hope to be loved in return. I learned at a young age that was a futile hope.

So I decided as young as late grammar school:

> "It's better for me to show my family I love them, even if no one loves me back.
>
> Love going in one direction is better than no one loving anyone at all."

This mindset set me on a horrifically destructive path that took me from one nightmare after another in my personal relationships. In each of them, I was sadly willing to give so much and ask for so little for myself. I had no understanding at all that my trying so hard to be kind, caring and forgiving only works in a relationship with a person who is healthy because that kind of person will not take advantage of my kindness. I had no clue that in a relationship with an unhealthy, abusive person all my willingness to be so kind and forgiving ends up being a huge mistake.

Change in this area only became possible when I realized that only seriously selfish people want to relate to someone in this one-sided way.

I had to also face that a healthy person is **not** going to be comfortable being mainly a taker in a relationship. He is not going to want me to do most of the caring, listening, and forgiving.

Rather I discovered that being kind, caring and forgiving is a beautiful way to be with a non-abusive person because rather than taking advantage of me being kind and caring, they only appreciate it and want to also relate to me in that same way.

The following insights helped me to understand how the Father feels about all this and seeing these insights was a huge part of me seeing all this in a new way:

> "Serve one another. Accept one another. Encourage each other. Love each other with genuine affection. Take delight in honoring each other. Have the same care for one another."
>
> 1 Corinthians 12:25, 2 Corinthians 13:11 NLT/NASB
> Romans 15:7, 12:10 NASB/NLT
> Galatians 5:13 NASB

Even the Apostle Paul expressed that he needed a two-way caring when he told the early church believers:

> **"I'm eager to encourage you.**
> **But I also want to be encouraged by you."**
> Romans 1:12 NLT/NCV

Amazingly, Jesus had this same need for two-way relationship.

He deeply loved His Team. But He also wanted them to give that same caring to Him.

That's why in the Garden He felt painfully alone.

He needed His close ones to be there for Him. But they were emotionally disconnected from what He was going through.

This grieved Him.

So He was honest about how hurtful their disconnect felt when He said to them: "Couldn't you just stay awake and be with Me during these moments I'm in such pain?" Yet when we make up our mind to grow and change and no longer accept what is totally unhealthy and destructively selfish, we finally get to experience the kind of mutually supportive, mutually caring personal relationships that the human soul longs for that is captured in this verse:

> "Two people can accomplish more than twice as much as one. And if one person falls, the other can reach out and help. But people who are alone when they fall are in real trouble. A person standing alone can be attacked and defeated but two can stand back to back and conquer."
>
> Ecclesiastes 4:9-12 NLT

This mutually supportive relationship is what we were designed by God to experience.

It's the kind of bond with another person that makes it possible for us to get through to the other side of the inevitable ups and downs of life and with an even greater understanding of one another and an even more rewarding, fulfilling closeness.

Chapter Eleven

CONTROL AND ABUSE

A controlling person can always be one step away from being abusive.

The mistreatment can be set off when a person realizes that he can no longer get you to do exactly what he wants. Then in his mind, you will be blamed for whatever occurs because to that person your resistant attitude toward their control is responsible for "making" them hurt you. Consequently, if you continue in any relationship that is significantly controlling, you are at risk of eventually experiencing emotional, physical, sexual or verbal abuse in that relationship.

These are some of the behaviors that indicate someone is controlling.

*In all cases "he" refers to **both** a woman or a man.*

His world revolves around his needs and his feelings.

So if something affects him, he is sensitive to it. It strongly matters to him. But what affects you and what you need are not as important to him.

You have to like what he thinks you should like. You have to do what he thinks you should do. You have to be who he thinks you should be. If you differ with him in any of these areas, his attitude will be that there's something wrong with you.

You have to do what he expects of you. Otherwise he is critical and disapproving. He communicates both verbally and nonverbally, in extremely hurtful ways, that you are a disappointment to him.

His words are at times unkind. This means he has the potential to speak words that are cruel and degrading.

He tries to control who your friends are. He does not want you to have relationships with those he doesn't want you to be close to.

If you make a decision he does not agree with, he is not pleased. He will not be supportive of what you have decided.

He gets angry if you express an insight or point of view that is different from his.

To be wrong in any disagreement means that he is losing some of his control. Therefore, being right is the most important thing to him. This causes him to be rigid and stubborn. As a result, healthy communication and loving solutions to disagreements are not possible.

Chapter Twelve

WE CAN'T CHANGE ANYONE ELSE

When I was still clueless about what I needed to notice in someone's behaviors as I began to get to know them, I was energized by "helping" them overcome their negative qualities. This always proved to be a disaster because seriously unhealthy people are often very good at making temporary changes in how they act.

But those changes always disappeared after I was seriously involved with them. At that point, they inevitably reverted back to acting like the person they actually are and the pain I began to experience in the relationship was familiar territory. So I still continued the relationship.

For example, this is how my husband acted when I was dating him:

He was secretive and stingy about money. But I was convinced that I would try so hard to be good to him that he would learn to be generous with me.

He was excessively nervous and troubled. Yet I decided I would be so understanding and kind that his nervousness would heal.

He became defensive at the slightest challenge to his thinking or behaviors. I looked at this as something he was doing because no one had ever loved him enough to help him feel that he was being listened to. So I told myself: "I see his potential as a person. If I am very kind to him and I keep loving him a lot, he will change."

He was stubborn. He had to be right. Everything had to be done his way or there was tension. What He wanted had to happen or he wasn't happy with me. But I told myself I had to learn to bend more his way in order to love him and keep things happy between us.

I felt sorry for him when he described all the ways he had been hurt by women. I saw him more like he was a hurting little boy than a grown man who was blaming others for his problems, while at the same time he didn't take any responsibility for them. I told myself that he just needed for me to be very good to him and he would get better. I didn't see that he actually did want me feeling sorry for him and he liked me mothering him and "taking care of" him in ways that no healthy man would ever want or accept.

He was oblivious to my needs and how I was feeling. If I explained to him something he did was hurtful, when it happened again he couldn't remember that I had ever told him. So I had to go through the same upsetting turmoil explaining it all again. As I did, it was as if I had never shared my hurt feelings with him at all.

Yet I made excuses for him by telling myself: "He has been single so long that he just needs my help to learn to be more understanding of my feelings."

In the face of all these issues, I just kept saying to myself: "He's got a lot of rough edges. But if I'm kind to him and if I encourage him, he will make the changes he needs for us to be happy."

I was foolishly convinced that his problem was that no one had ever encouraged him enough to help him develop to his full potential.

So he became my project to love into being who I needed him to be. And he did become quite different during the months before our wedding day. However, all that quickly disappeared after we were married.

This is who he became after our wedding:

His secretiveness and stinginess turned into him being rigidly controlling over every detail of my use of money. His constantly watching closely what I was spending became more and more stressful for me. This caused so much tension between us that it began to affect me physically. Dealing with all this emotional turmoil became a way of life for me.

His nervousness never improved. It actually became much worse. All the things I had been convinced would help him overcome it proved to be completely useless.

His obliviousness to how I was feeling never changed. He could only connect emotionally to what affected him, no matter how many times I told him how hurt I felt.

He believed he had a right to be harsh with me. He would often say, "The Bible tells you to respect me. It does not tell me I have to respect you."

When I told him he was hurtful, he justified being cruel by telling me that I deserved it because I wouldn't do whatever he said was important to him. Therefore I was selfish. I became so beat down emotionally by his many criticisms of me that I told myself more and more frequently: "I must be the problem. So I have to somehow try harder to be more loving and caring about his needs.

He never could remember what I told him was deeply hurtful in our relationship. Days later it was as if I had said nothing at all. This "forgetting" made it easy for him to justify the same hurtful treatment toward me and my children.

He insisted that things be done his way. He harshly insisted that the Bible only tells the wife to respect the husband.

He did not believe that the Bible ever tells the husband to also respect the wife.

He insisted on absolute obedience to his authority over me. He justified this by using his interpretation of the verses in the Bible about a wife's submission. He also used this place of power and control to make decisions that met his needs, but neglected mine.

Any moment I had a different perspective from him, it turned into a volatile flare up of his verbally degrading anger.

To avoid his defensiveness, I complied more and more with his insistence that I agree with his demands that I do want he wanted and decided.

I felt less and less safe being honest with him about any of my feelings or about any of my thinking that did not agree with him.

His hatred toward women eventually included me and my daughter.

Ever since I experienced this disillusioning heartache I have not allowed myself to forget that I can never change anyone else. I only have the ability to choose how I am going to change myself.

Consequently I realized that I either have peace and joy in knowing someone and being with them, or they are a mistake for me to have a close, personal relationship with.

Chapter Thirteen

BEHAVIORS AND TRUTH

When you are getting to know unhealthy people, they are often excellent talkers who are highly skilled in manipulation.

You can only know who people really are when you look past their words and carefully observe if their behaviors line up with what they say.

I learned this wisdom the hard way because from a young age, my relationship with my mother "taught" me **not** to base who I think a person really is on how they act, but only on the **words** they speak.

She insisted that I believe she loved me. Yet her words never matched her cold, rejecting behaviors. At my slightest reluctance to believe her, she insisted, "You know I do."

I then was required to accept that if she **said** she loved me, she did, no matter how much her actions didn't line up at all with her words.

As I grew older, I took this conditioning into my relationships with those I dated. Consequently, when I was getting to know anyone, if they told me they loved me, I just went along with what they said. I accepted that it was true. I deeply regretted the world of pain that this huge mistake caused me.

Yet when I became determined to stop having personal relationships with unhealthy people, I realized that I could never again accept anyone's words as the accurate picture of who they are.

The Father helped me to understand that I needed to make this major change in my thinking when I found this scripture:

"Stop just saying you love each other. Really show it by your actions. It is by your actions that you will know you are living in the truth."

1 John 3:18-19 NLT

Once I realized that this was how I needed to think, I was also just as affected by the Word warning me:

**"Violent people deceive their companions,
leading them down a harmful path."**
Proverbs 16:29 NLT

Due to my long, mixed up history of being clueless, naïve, gullible and easily deceived when it came to seeing people for who they really are, I was also relieved to discover that God made this promise:

**"Come and listen to my counsel.
I'll share my heart with you and make you wise."**
Proverbs 1:23 NLT

So I often come to the Father for His wisdom and insights about relationships and He is always very happy to help me and show me "stuff" I never saw before. That's why, I've learned along this Journey of getting more and more free that one of the best prayers for me to ever say when I am wondering about anything is:

"Father! Help!

Then what is captured in these priceless words becomes amazingly possible:

"What wings are to a bird and sails to a ship, so is prayer to the soul." *Corrie Ten Boom*

I also get to experience these rock solid promises happening:

"When I pray the Father answers me. He encourages me by giving me the strength I need. While I am still praying He actually sends His answer to me." "

Psalm 138:3 NLT, Isaiah 65:24 NASB

Yet, despite all this growing and learning about how to become more and more free, and though I am quick to ask God to help me see what I need to understand, sometimes I still "miss it." At times I don't see accurately if someone is a healthy person to have a personal relationship with.

But the **really good news** is that these mistakes don't happen as often because I've gotten better and better at being willing to listen to the Father when He's trying to warn me.

It is this listening to Him that can hugely protect *anyone* from making serious errors about who to be close friends with, who to date, and who to marry.

Chapter Fourteen

CHOICES VS. BLAMING

It's tragic when children are abused. They are helpless, innocent victims. But when we become adults, people can only do to us what we **allow** them to do.

To clarify, there are traumatic things that happen to young people and adults over which they have no control, such as when a person is raped. These are victims who must not feel responsible for what was forced on them. So when I say that after we grow up then people can only do to us what we let them do, I'm referring to blaming our adult problems on what someone did to us when we can **choose** to not allow it.

For example, all the suffering I experienced beginning when I was a young adult only became possible because of my own extremely twisted, sick decision to **accept** being mistreated. That's why it was such a serious mistake for me to tell myself when an abusive relationship ended:

> "I just got rid of my problem.
> He is out of my life. Now I will be happy."

Blaming my problems on someone else meant that I had not faced the fact that it was my allowing that made all the abuse possible and also because I was so unhealthy inside of me, this is why really unhealthy people were drawn to me.

Therefore, I would inevitably end up in another destructive relationship with someone who was incapable of loving me.

I am the one who had to change what was going on inside of me before this horribly negative pattern could finally end.

What helped this to become possible is I pleaded with the Father to please show me:

Why have I always been attracted to cruel people?
Why have they always been attracted to me?

That's when He gladly helped me to see I must be willing to admit that my mixed up life as an adult **wasn't** someone else's fault.

Rather the problems I had experienced came from me letting others do things to me that I should **never allow** and the **only** person who could stop this sick, destructive "allowing" was me.

That was an unsettling revelation.

It was not fun at all to face.

Yet looking at myself honestly, instead of seeing others as the reason for my problems was also the beginning of some seriously needed growing that had to happen before I could ever find my way to emotional freedom.

Chapter Fifteen

HEALTHY VS. UNHEALTHY

An unhealthy person typically feels that somehow it's our responsibility to do something to make them happy.

Yet happiness is something we each need to find within our own heart and from our own choices in life. No one can "make" us happy. They can add joy, fun, fulfillment, inspiration and encouragement.

But people can't cause us to be happy if in our own heart we are "down" a lot and often feel negative about people and life.

This insight is exactly what this quote is referring to:

"Happiness isn't something that depends on our surroundings. It's something we make inside ourselves." *Corrie Ten Boom*

Before I learned this valuable area of wisdom, I was a magnet for anyone who was hurting.

They always wanted me to do something to help them not to be in so much pain. They wanted my upbeat ability to be encouraging and caring to "help" them feel happy.

As a result, I allowed friends and those I was dating to need me in unhealthy ways. I actually defined love as someone **needing** me to help them feel better about themselves. When I became a Christian, I continued live like this. Only now I thought I was following God's command to love when I related to people in this seriously unhealthy way.

Eventually I learned from the Bible that this was not a good way to think at all. This is how the Father helped me to see this surprising, hugely important insight.

His Word tells us:

"Bear one another's burdens."
Galatians 6:2 NASB

This caring and suffering with others who are hurting was nothing new to me. It was actually a way of life for me that was all mixed up.

But what began to change the way I related to people was realizing that only three verses later this statement seemed to contradict my unhealthy way of thinking:

"Each one shall bear his own load."
Galatians 6:5 NASB

The Father was trying to help us understand in those two verses is that He **does** want us to care about people when they are suffering.

But He also wants us to have His practical wisdom about when a person needs to work out their own issues and problems and not lean on us emotionally or financially to help them.

I had no clue how to find this balance for the longest time because a lot of what I used to think was me being kind and loving was actually me fulfilling my need to feel "needed." Seeing this greatly helped me. It opened up invaluable understanding when I was reaching out to love someone for the Father. It hugely changed who I wanted to be close to as a friend.

It also was very encouraging to discover that healthy people **want** a personal relationship to be mutual.

They **don't** want the basis of our closeness to be them leaning on me emotionally or them being "needy." As a result, I began to experience wonderful, inspiring, genuinely encouraging people being drawn to me because they sense that this is how I feel also.

All these remarkable changes still feel like a giant ***"Wow!"*** to me.

Chapter Sixteen

"I HAVEN'T CHANGED ENOUGH!"

These are some of the ways that you can tell you will still be attracted to an unhealthy person. Likewise, if this is still who you are, people who are a mistake for you to get personally involved with will still really "like" you.

The list...

You want someone to feel sorry for you.

You are so insecure within yourself that you need constant emotional support like a child would need and this makes you an exhausting person for anyone who is emotionally healthy to be closely involved with.

You are frequently overwhelmed by handling just the normal challenges of life.

You want to lean heavily on others to help you solve your problems. You can't face that it's your extreme emotional "neediness" that is the reason why others are not comfortable helping you more.

You make excuses for your unhealthy behaviors.

You also make excuses for the unkind, inconsiderate, rude, selfish, stingy behaviors of others.

You are way too willing to give too much for what another person needs or wants.

You want way too much to feel needed by another person. As a result you will attract people who will gladly lean on you in unhealthy ways for their needs to be met.

You like to mother adults. So people who want you to "take care of them" will be strongly drawn to you.

You are willing to do most of the giving and caring in a friendship or with someone you are dating. Consequently selfish, emotionally unavailable, abusive people will be drawn to you like a giant magnet.

You dwell on the past. Yet a healthy person does not want a personal relationship with someone who has to think and talk about their past hurts, betrayals or abuse.

You haven't learned to say to yourself and mean it when you are suffering in a personal relationship: "This doesn't feel good. I deserve better. It isn't supposed to hurt like this when I am with someone who says they care about me."

You have not learned to be honest about your true feelings and your own needs. As a result, you will easily attract people who are rigid, stubborn, selfish, emotionally abusive, and are perfectly fine with being oblivious to your feelings and needs.

You still hesitate to be honest when you are uncomfortable or you disagree. As a result, abusive people will be strongly attracted to your unwillingness to share your honest feelings because this allows them to be demanding, selfish and controlling, all with a minimum amount of hassles from you.

Unhealthy people are still drawn to your willingness to be kind, caring and quick to forgive because they can sense that you are willing for a personal relationship to be one-sided. Somehow they know from the way you relate to people that you are someone whose good heart can be taken advantage of.

Chapter Seventeen

"WOW!
I HAVE CHANGED!"

What I've experienced is that if the list below describes who you are, then most unhealthy people are **not** going to enjoy getting to know you.

The list...

You like who you are.

You are not looking for someone to "rescue" you from your problems. In fact, you don't want anything to do with that mindset.

You have developed a healthy level of independence.

You have developed your own interests and hobbies.

You have your own dreams and goals and you are taking practical steps toward accomplishing them.

You have the ability to be content when you are alone.

You can enjoy using time by yourself in positive and rewarding ways.

You have forgiven everyone who has ever been hurtful to you.

You realize you can't change what happened to you in the past. You don't even want to think or talk about the past.

You want to move forward with what God has for you in the present and in His "future and hope" for you.

You are convinced that you do have the power to choose how you will respond to life and people.

You are encouraging. But you don't feel a responsibility to make someone else happy even if they expect you to do that.

You can watch a person you care about struggle, and be supportive. But you don't feel it is your responsibility to "fix" their pain. If they try to lean on you emotionally with the expectation that you should "help" them, you back off from that personal relationship.

There are times in any relationship when the caring will go toward one person more than the other and this is healthy. But you don't feel it's selfish to want the loving and supporting in a personal relationship to go both directions. Instead you've made up your mind that this is what you really want and need in order to be someone's close friend or in order to date someone.

You no longer allow any friend or anyone you are dating to be unkind to you. You also don't make excuses for someone if they are selfish, rude or unkind.

If you are drawn to someone, it's because you like that person just the way they are. There's nothing about them that you feel you need to "work on" to help them change.

You want to be with someone whom you can have fun with and laugh with. Therefore those who are healthy will really find you fun to be with. They will be drawn to experiencing mutual, rewarding relationship with you.

Unhealthy people are no longer drawn to your willingness to be kind, caring and quick to forgive because they can sense that you are unwilling for a personal relationship to be one-sided. Somehow they know from the way you relate to people that you are not willing for your caring heart to be taken advantage of. And if they do end up wanting to connect with you, you can "see" what's happening and you are not willing to have a personal relationship with them.

***

After I became someone who lives and thinks in these new ways, there were moments that were really hard on me. I longed for kindred people to come into my life that I could have a close personal relationship with.

This is one of those difficult moments that I vividly recall:

I knelt in front of the couch in the living room where I now lived by myself and buried my face in my arms.

I longed to have someone love me and treat me with kindness. I wanted so much to have my first friendship that was based on my new, Word-based thinking.

"Please help me, Lord," I cried out. "Please help me."

Gently, the Father reminded me of this promise He always spoke to me when I struggled:

**"Delight yourself in Me and
I will give you the desires of your heart.**

**Commit your way to Me and
trust Me and I will do it."**
Psalm 37:4-5 NASB

I knew I had to once again give to the Father my need to be loved. So I told Him with a lot of tears:

"I lay down this tremendous ache in my heart. I give it to You, all over again and I choose to believe that You will give me the desires of my heart. But please help me to find my way back to Your comforting peace."

In response to that cry of my heart God always restored me and He did that with much reassuring kindness and comfort.

That was many years ago.

He kept His promise. He ***did*** give me the desires of my heart.

What's amazing to me is that ever since I was a little girl, I was alone any time I fell down in life. There was never anyone there to help me get back up again.

But now I'm experiencing genuinely mutual, healthy relationships. We are there for each other. When one of us is down, the other encourages, just like is described in Ecclesiastes 4:9:

> "Two people can accomplish more than twice as much as one. And if one person falls, the other can reach out and help. But people who are alone when they fall are in real trouble and can be attacked and defeated. But two can stand back to back and conquer."

All that God has done for me, He longs to do for each of His children. That's why He promises us:

"I know the plans I have for you.
They are for good and not destruction.
To give you a future and a hope."
Jeremiah 29:11

He's just like the Dad in this true Story

In 1989, an 8.2 earthquake almost flattened Armenia, killing over 30,000 people in less than four minutes. In the midst of utter devastation and chaos, a father left his wife securely at home and rushed to the school where his son was supposed to be.

That's when he discovered that the building was as flat as a pancake.

After the traumatic initial shock, he remembered the promise he had made to his son: "No matter what, I'll always be there for you!"

Tears began to fill his eyes. As he looked at the pile of debris that once was the school, it looked hopeless, but he kept remembering his commitment to his son. He began to concentrate on where he walked his son to class at school each morning. Remembering that his son's classroom would be in the back right corner of the building, he rushed there and started digging through the rubble.

As he was digging, other forlorn parents arrived, clutching their hearts, saying: "My son!" "My daughter!"

Other well-meaning parents tried to pull him off of what was left of the school saying:

"It's too late!"

"They're dead!"

"You can't help!"

"Go home!"

"Come on, face reality, there's nothing you can do! You're just going to make things worse!"

To each parent he responded with one line: "Are you going to help me now?"

Then he proceeded to dig for his son, stone by stone.

Soon the fire chief showed up and tried to pull him off of the school's debris. He told this father, "Fires are breaking out, explosions are everywhere. You are in danger. We'll take care of it. Go home."

To which this loving, caring Armenian father asked, "Are you going to help me now?"

The police came and said, "You're angry, distraught and it's over. You're endangering others. Go home. We'll handle it!" To which he replied, "Are you going to help me now?"

No one helped. Courageously he proceeded alone. He needed to know for himself: "Is my boy alive or is he dead?"

He kept digging and in the 38th hour as he pulled back a boulder he heard his son's voice.

He screamed his son's name, "Armand!" and heard back, "Dad!? It's me, Dad!" the boy cried out. "I told the other kids not to worry. I told them that if you were alive, you'd save me and when you saved me, they'd be saved. You promised me that no matter what, you'll always be there for me! And you did it, Dad!"

"What's going on in there? How is it?" the father asked.

"There are fourteen of us left out of thirty-three, Dad. We're scared, hungry, thirsty and thankful you're here. When the building collapsed, it made a wedge, like a triangle, and it saved us."

"Come on out, boy!"

"No, Dad! Let the other kids out first, because I know you'll get me! No matter what, I know you'll be there for me!"

Taken from "Chicken Soup for the Soul"
1999 Father's Day Message

God used this story to further help me see how much He wants us to feel safe and secure in His love:

"A young girl traveling on a train for the first time heard that it would have to cross several rivers. She was troubled and fearful as she thought of the water. But each time the train came to a river, a bridge was always there to provide a safe way across it.

After passing safely over several rivers and streams, the girl settled back in her seat with a sigh of relief. Then she turned to her mother and said, 'I'm not worried anymore. Somebody has put bridges for us all of the way.'"

Corrie Ten Boom

Just as soon as I read those words, this is how the Father encouraged me.

"My Child,

I will do the same for you as I did for that young child on the train.

During any moments that are troubling or scary for you, I am always here to provide an unexpected bridge for you so that you can relax inside and be at peace.

So please.

Take My hand.

Let Me help you.

I promise you as your Father that I will turn your Valley of heartbreaking losses and griefs into a life-changing Door of Hope.

I will show you the way to your freedom.

- Your Dad who cares about you with a love you can depend on all the days of your life, no matter what"

SOURCES

ANOTHER BOOK BY THE AUTHOR

REVIVAL ON THE HORIZON

Revival is not about a new truth being revealed. It's always the restoration of a lost truth that the Father longs for His people to earnestly care about once again. It is a Radical Transformation in a child of God which changes our character so that we can carry the presence of God and His love everywhere we go, just like happened when Christianity was birthed. This is why there is a desperate need in this hour for an Awakening to the truths of love and unity that in the early church "turned the world upside down." Acts 17:6 AMP That taking place drew in the unsaved as they witnessed a genuine love and an unselfish unity between the new believers that they had never seen before.

Then down through the ages, the story of God's people has been about the ache in the Father's heart for these radically life-changing truths to be restored to His church.

This book is filled with hope for the generations about Revival not only being possible, but what it is going to take for it to continue when it does ignite. Its passionate message grips the heart. It moves to tears. It pierces the soul with the fire of God. It equips believers in extraordinarily practical, simple ways how they can be part of the unprecedented move of God that the Father is longing to pour out across the nations. All of this is why "Revival on the Horizon" is a powerful, seriously needed book with a timely message for this hour in the history of Christianity.

ABOUT THE MINISTRY

OUR VISION

Revival igniting and spreading as a Holy Fire across generations, denominations and nations

Restoration of the love and unity that exploded in the Book of Acts Revival and changed the world

Impartation of Prophetic Ministry to inspire young and old to enter into God's destiny for them

Miraculous transformations, supernatural healings that set people free

Helping a fatherless younger generation know God as a loving Dad

Humble from the heart worship, intimately encountering God in a Visitation of His presence

TO CONTACT THE MINISTRY

If you are interested in getting more information about who we are and what we do, please visit us online at www.lighthouse-of-hope.org. Also if you would like to inquire about having Ruth and Barry come to your group to minister, please send an email to ruth@lighthouse-of-hope.org or barry@lighthouse-of-hope.org, or call us at 425-775-3904.

www.lighthouse-of-hope.org

facebook.com/LighthouseOfHopeMinistries

49865718R00089

Made in the USA
Charleston, SC
04 December 2015